KiDSavvy™ Westchester

A parents' guide of information & inspiration

Betsy Cadel and Laura E. Wilker

D1367698

SUBURBAN GODDESS PRESS, INC., HARTSDALE, NY

Cover design and illustration by Greg Paprocki (www.gregpaprocki.com)
Book design by Cathy Solarana (www.visuallyspeaking.biz)
Author photo by Lori Sherman

LCCN 2003091292
ISBN 0-9727477-0-2

Publisher's Note
Neither Suburban Goddess nor the authors have any interest, financial, personal or otherwise, in the locations and services listed in this book. No fees were paid or services rendered in exchange for inclusion in these pages. While every effort was made to ensure that information regarding phone numbers, hours, admission fees and prices was complete and accurate at the time of publication, it is always best to call ahead and verify. Any slights of people, places or organizations are unintentional. We recommend that readers discuss all health-related issues with their medical practitioner before acting.

Acknowledgements

A book like this doesn't happen without the help and input of lots and lots of people. Thank you to all the people who have been such generous sources of information and support, especially Wendy, Elise, Randi, Alisa and Dana, and to all the friends who helped us research and experience all that Westchester has to offer. To Leyla, our eagle-eyed editor, whose speed and great attitude impressed us to no end. To Cathy, our art director, whose creativity and hard work brought our hard work to life. Most of all, lots of love and thanks to "our boys"— Andrew and Sam, Andy and Simon—who were so patient with all our working weekends. We couldn't have done this without you. We love you more than words can say.

A special thanks to Betsy's mom, Lyna Zommick, a "Savvy Supporter" whose generosity and encouragement have meant so much, and to our consummate cheerleaders June and Marty.

This book is dedicated to the memories of Muriel Wilker, Roberta Oliner, Dr. Simon Levin and Dr. Sidney Wilker. You were our role models in writing, parenting, and everything in between. How much fun you would have had exploring Westchester with your grandchildren! We miss you.

table of contents

table of contents

table of contents

i'm here! now what?

Whether you migrated to Westchester with several children already, with a bulging belly, or even with just with your husband in tow, chances are you moved here because you heard it was a wonderful place to raise kids. And it is. We both left New York City and moved here before getting pregnant, thinking we'd get to know "the lay of the land" before becoming parents. Within a few years the babies came and we realized we hadn't just given birth to a brand-new life: we'd given birth to a brand-new lifestyle.

We wondered, "Why do we feel so isolated in an area that's full of families?" We tried the usual routes to stave off new-mother insanity. Laura did laps at the mall with her "Hummer"-sized stroller. While she awkwardly pushed Sam through aisles of clothes she was sure she'd never fit into again, she was being pushed to the brink. Betsy signed up for a bunch of classes that were meant to enrich her pudgy little bundle of joy, but he was barely old enough to shake a rattle, let alone a maraca. What can we say? We were desperate. We commiserated about how surprisingly difficult it was to figure out such a supposedly family-friendly place. Unlike our "sisters in the city," most of us didn't have

1

Savvy Suggestion
The Perfectly Packed Diaper Bag
* Diapers
* Burp cloths
* Baby wipes
* Rash ointment
* Hand-sanitizing gel
* Change of baby clothes
* Receiving blanket
* Nursing pads or extra bottle/nipple/formula
* Bottled water
* Extra pacifier
* Plastic bags
* A clean shirt and a snack for you

Savvy Suggestion

Go to the local Real Estate office and ask for a map of the area. They tend to be extremely detailed yet very easy to read. Get two copies so that you can keep one in your house and one in a folder in your car.

play dates an apartment away. We couldn't just toss our little ones in strollers and have immediate access to dozens of playgrounds, stores, restaurants and, most importantly, other moms.

Eventually, like all moms do, we created our own little network of contacts, friends and activities. We had playgroups, preschool and classes galore—but we also still had lots of questions. Where should Betsy go to get Simon's first haircut? Where should Laura buy Sam's first "big boy" bed?

A trip to the local bookstore proved to be an exercise in futility. Countless volumes *(often in second, third and fourth editions)* have been written to help our urban counterparts navigate this new life with a child, but no book existed to help us suburban moms.

We wanted a simple way to find out about all that Westchester has to offer. Preferably it would be one central resource, with entries listed by town. And, if it wasn't too much trouble, some advice on things like original ideas for birthday parties and where to go on a rainy afternoon would be nice. We wanted what all suburban moms want *(besides a good night's sleep)*: we wanted information at our fingertips. With all the other things we have to do, who has time to play detective when it comes to finding play spaces?

They say necessity is the mother of invention. And so *KidSavvy Westchester* was born. You are holding the ultimate insider's listing of classes, indoor play spaces, parks, museums, stores, useful websites and more. The entries are followed by comprehensive descriptions, including locations, phone numbers, age-appropriateness and special "What to Know Before

You Go" sections with tips you won't find anywhere else. We've done the homework for you. Even the most "seasoned" mom will find useful information in these pages. And you'll also find dozens of "Savvy Suggestions," "Savvy Savings" and "Savvy Superlatives" throughout the book that will give you advice, ideas and cost-saving tips.

Savvy Suggestion

If you are a member of AAA, take advantage of the free book of New York maps they offer. They're the clearest and easiest-to-follow maps we've found. There is a AAA office located at 111 Brook Street in Scarsdale, or you can check their website at www.aaany.com.

We found that being a mom in the suburbs *(or a Suburban Goddess, as we like to say)* requires a lot of planning, a good map and many trips in and out of car seats. But, truly, Westchester has so much to offer, both for kids and for parents. We hope this book helps make your life not only more fun but also a little bit easier.

While we've made every attempt to make sure that everything out *there* is in *here*, we're certain that we've missed some things. Let us know—we'd love to hear from you!—and we'll add them to the next edition. Please e-mail us at **suburbangoddess@kidsavvy.net** or visit **www.kidsavvy.net**.

Enjoy!

the grass is always greener

Community Playgrounds
County & State Parks
Gardens & Other Gorgeous Places
Nature Centers & Preserves
Other Outdoor Attractions

It seems that one of the first things every new mom discovers is her local playground. It's a place to get some fresh air, to meet other moms and, as your children grow, to let them burn off some energy while having a lot of fun. Then one day it will hit you: you're bored with a capital "B." You are now officially ready to start exploring other options. The good news is that Westchester is all about beautiful outdoor spaces.

So whether you're looking for a wonderful place for a stroll, a fun day at a nature center, or just a different swing set and slide, look no further. We've also included information you'll need to know about each location, such as the facilities, the types of activities available and whether there is an admission fee.

Community Playgrounds

The following sites all have playgrounds, but the facilities vary widely—some have multiple systems of play equipment for different age groups, while others have just a swing set. We've also listed whatever additional features these sites have, whether it's paths for you to walk with your infant in a backpack, fields for your new runner to practice his skills, places to picnic or grill, or ice-skating or swimming facilities.

Many of these playgrounds also offer children's programs such as educational events, entertainment and summer camp.

These playgrounds are run by specific municipalities—that is, by cities, towns or villages *(hamlets are included within the towns)*. Virtually all of them are open to the public, but some require a municipal park pass or only admit residents from the specific municipality. For more playgrounds, see other sections of this chapter; almost all of the county and state parks have playgrounds, as do the Blue Mountain and Ward Pound Ridge Reservations *(listed in the "Nature Centers & Preserves" section of this chapter)*.

ARDSLEY
* Anthony F. Veteran Park *(11 Olympic Ln.)*—picnicking/ grills, refreshments, swimming
* Ashford Park *(Ashford Ave.)*—fields, picnicking
* McDowell Park *(Heatherdell Rd.)*—fields, picnicking

BEDFORD
* Bedford Hills Park *(Haines Rd.)*—fields, picnicking, swimming
* Bedford Memorial Park *(Greenwich Rd., Bedford Village)* —fields, ice-skating, picnicking, swimming
* Katonah Memorial Park *(North St., Katonah)*—fields, hiking/walking, picnicking, sledding, swimming

BRIARCLIFF MANOR
* Chilmark Park *(Macy Rd.)*—fields
* Jackson Road Park *(Jackson Rd.)*
* Law Memorial Park *(Pleasantville Rd.)*—swimming, wading pool
* Neighborhood Park *(Whitson & Fuller Rds.)*—fields

BRONXVILLE
* Dogwood Park *(Garden Ave.)*
* Sagamore Park *(Sagamore Rd.)*
* School Field *(Bronxville Public School)*—fields

BUCHANAN
* Recreation Site *(West Ave.)*—fields, swimming

CORTLANDT
* Buchanan/Verplanck Elementary School *(Westchester Ave., Verplanck)*
* Charles J. Cook Recreation Center *(Furnace Dock Rd.)* —fields, picnicking/grills, swimming
* Frank G. Lindsey Elementary School *(Trolley Rd., Montrose)*—fields
* Lake Allendale Playground *(Allen Rd.)*
* Maple Avenue Playground *(Lafayette & Maple Aves.)*
* Muriel H. Morabito Community Center *(Westbrook Dr.)*
* Sprout Brook Park *(Sprout Brook Rd.)*—picnicking/grills, swimming
* Sunset Park *(Montrose Point Rd., Montrose)*—fields
* Tommy Thurber Playground *(Tommy Thurber Ln., off Sunset)*

CROTON-ON-HUDSON
* Dobbs Park *(Maple St., Rte. 129)*—fields
* Duck Pond Park *(Bungalow Rd., off S. Riverside Ave.)* —fields
* Senasqua Park *(on the Hudson River)*—picnicking
* Sunset Park *(Sunset & Lexington Drs.)*

DOBBS FERRY
* Gould Park *(Ashford Ave.)*—fields, swimming
* Memorial Park *(Palisade St.)*—fields, wading pool
* Waterfront Park *(on the Hudson River)* —picnicking/grills *(open to Dobbs Ferry residents only)*

EASTCHESTER
* Chester Heights Park *(Oregon Ave.)*—fields
* Cooper Field *(Locust Ave.)*—fields, tot lot
* Garth Road Park *(Garth Rd.)*—fields, picnicking
* Joyce Road Park *(Joyce Rd.)*—fields
* Leewood Park *(Leewood Dr.)*—fields

ELMSFORD
* Massaro Park *(50 Cabot Ave.)*—fields, picnicking/grills, swimming
* Pocantico Park *(Saw Mill River Rd.)*—picnicking/grills

GREENBURGH
* Secor Woods Park *(Secor Rd., Hartsdale)*—fields, picnicking/ grills
* Webb Park *(Central Ave., Hartsdale)*—fields, picnicking

HARRISON
* Bernie Guagnini Brentwood Park *(Webster Ave.)*— picnicking, swimming, wading pool
* Congress Park *(Congress St.)*—fields
* John Passidomo Veteran Park *(Lake St., W. Harrison)*— fields, picnicking, refreshments, swimming, wading pool
* Pettijohn Park *(Crotona Ave. & Avondale Rd.)*
* Riis Park/Station Park *(Harrison Ave. & Heineman Pl.)*
* Rose Avenue Tot Lot *(Rose Ave.)*
* Veterans Memorial Park *(Crystal St.)*—fields, hiking/ walking, picnicking
* Wilding Park *(Oakland Ave.)*—picnicking

HASTINGS-ON-HUDSON
* MacEchron Waterfront Park *(on the Hudson River)*— picnicking
* Reynolds Field *(Chauncey Ln.)*—fields
* Uniontown Field *(Rose St.)*—fields, picnicking

IRVINGTON
* Scenic Hudson Park at Irvington *(Bridge St., on the Hudson River)*—fields, hiking/walking, picnicking *(open to Irvington residents only between Memoral Day & Labor Day, but the guard leaves at 5 pm so enjoy!)*
* Taxter Road Park *(21 Taxter Rd.)*

LARCHMONT
* Flint Park *(Locust Ave., off Thompson St.)*—fields, picnicking
* Pinebrook Park *(Palmer)*
* Turtle Park *(Palmer, near train station)*
* Willow Park *(Willow Ave., off the beach)*—fields

LEWISBORO
* Onatru Farm Park *(99 Elmwood Rd., South Salem)*— fields, hiking/walking
* Town Park *(Rte. 35, South Salem)*—fields, hiking/walking, ice-skating, picnicking, swimming

MAMARONECK
* **Hommocks Park Ice Rink & Swimming Pool Complex** *(Hommocks Rd. & Rte. 1)*—ice-skating, swimming
* **Memorial Park** *(Myrtle Blvd.)*

MOUNT KISCO
* **Leonard Park & Memorial Pool** *(Main St.)*—picnicking, swimming
* **Mt. Kisco Community Center** *(Maple Ave.)*
* **Smith Park** *(Pineview Rd.)*—fields

MOUNT VERNON
* **Brush Park** *(W. 7th St. between S. 3rd St. & Union Ave.)*—fields, picnicking, refreshments
* **Eddie Williams Playground** *(7th Ave. between 3rd & 4th Sts.)*
* **Fleetwood Playground** *(E. Broad St. & Fleetwood Ave., Fleetwood)*
* **Fourth Street Park** *(W. 4th St. between S. 7th & 8th Aves.)*
* **Grove Street Playground** *(Grove St.)*
* **Hartley Park** *(Gramatan Ave. between Oakley & Lincoln Aves.)*
* **Howard St. Playground** *(High & Howard Sts.)*
* **Hutchinson Field** *(Garden Ave. & Sargent Pl.)*—fields, miniature golf, refreshments, skating
* **Lorraine Avenue Playground** *(Lorraine Ave. & Claremont Pl.)*
* **Memorial Field** *(Garden Ave. & Sandford Blvd.)*—fields, picnicking
* **Nichols School Playground** *(High St.)*
* **Old 7th Avenue Playground** *(7th Ave. between 2nd & 4th Sts.)*
* **Purdy Park** *(S. 9th Ave. & 2nd St.)*
* **Scouts Field** *(Midland & Gramatan Aves.)*
* **Sophie J. Mee Playground** *(S. 3rd Ave. & Sandford Blvd.)*

NEW CASTLE
* **Gedney Park** *(Rte. 133)*—fields, hiking/walking, ice-skating, picnicking, sledding
* **Millwood Park** *(half a mile north of the Taconic Parkway/Rte. 100 intersection, Millwood)*—fields, picnicking
* **Recreation Field/Back of Town Hall** *(200 S. Greeley Ave., Chappaqua)*—fields

NEW ROCHELLE

* D'Onofrio Park *(Emmet Terr.)*—fields, picnicking/grills
* Eddie Foy Park *(Pelham Rd., at Weyman Ave.)*
* Feeney Park *(7th St. & Washington Ave.)*—flower garden, hiking/walking
* Five Islands Park *(Le Fevre Ln., off Main St.)*—hiking/ walking, picnicking/grills
* Flower's Park/City Park *(City Park Rd., off Fifth Ave.)*— fields, picnicking, swimming
* Hudson Park *(Hudson Park Rd., off Pelham Rd.)*—refresh- ments, swimming beach
* Huguenot Park *(North Ave. & Eastchester Rd.)*—hiking/ walking, ice-skating
* Lincoln Park *(Lincoln Ave.)*—fields, swimming, wading pool
* Maplewood Park *(Ralph Rd.)*
* Pinebrook Park *(Pinebrook Blvd. & Tulip Ln.)*—fields
* Roosevelt Park *(Disbrow Ln.)*
* Seacord Park *(Allard Ave. & John St.)*
* Stephenson Park *(Stephenson Blvd.)*
* Sycamore Park *(King's Highway)*—fields
* VFW Tot Lot *(Pelham Rd. & Meadow Ln.)*

NORTH CASTLE

* Clove Road Park *(N. Broadway & Clove Rd., North White Plains)*—fields
* John A. Lombardi Park *(85 Cox Ave.)*—fields, picnicking
* North Castle Community Park *(205 Business Park Dr., Armonk)*—fields, hiking/walking, picnicking
* Quarry Park *(Old Orchard St., Quarry Heights)*
* Wallace Pond *(Rte. 22, Armonk)*
* Winkler Park *(Greenwich-Banksville Rd.)*

NORTH SALEM

* Joe Bohrdrum Park *(Sunset Drive & Daniel Road)*—fields, picnicking

OSSINING

* Buck Johnson Park *(Blue Lantern Rd.)*
* Gerlach Park *(Old Albany Post Rd.)*—fields, hiking/ walking, picnicking
* Louis Engel Waterfront Park *(adjacent to train station parking lot)*—picnicking

* **Ryder Park** *(Morningside Dr.)*—fields, hiking/walking, picnicking
* **Veterans Park** *(Narragansett Ave.)*—fields, picnicking

PELHAM
* **Julien's Playground** *(6th St. & 4th Ave.)*

PLEASANTVILLE
* **Nannahagen Park** *(Lake St.)*—swimming
* **Rossell Park** *(Rossell St.)*
* **Soldiers & Sailors Playground** *(Clark St. & Manville Rd.)*

PORT CHESTER
* **Edgewood Park** *(Grace Church St.)*
* **Lyon Park** *(Putnam Ave. & King St.)*
* **Recreation Park** *(Locust Ave.)*

POUND RIDGE
* **Town Park** *(Rte. 137)*—fields, picnicking/grills, swimming

RYE
* **Disbrow Park** *(Oakland Beach Ave.)*—fields
* **Gagliardo Park** *(Nursery Ln.)*—fields, picnicking
* **Recreation Park** *(281 Midland Ave.)*—fields, picnicking

RYE BROOK
* **Crawford Park** *(Ridge St.)*—fields, picnicking
* **Garibaldi Park** *(Garibaldi Pl.)*—fields
* **Pine Ridge Park** *(Pine Ridge Rd.)*—fields

SCARSDALE
* **Aspen Park** *(Aspen Rd.)*—fields
* **Corell Park** *(East of Corell Rd. at Sycamore Rd.)*—fields
* **Crossway Field** (Mamaroneck Rd. & Crossway)—fields
* **Davis Park** *(Lyons Rd. & Grand Blvd.)*—fields
* **Greenacres Playground** *(Huntington Ave. & Montrose Rd.)*
* **Hyatt Field** *(Boulevard & Potter Rd.)*—fields
* **Municipal Pool** *(Mamaroneck Rd.)*—refreshments, swimming
* **Scout/Butler Field** *(Wayside Ln.)*—fields

SLEEPY HOLLOW
* Barnhart Park *(Barnhart Ave.)*
* Devries Park *(Devries Ave.)*—fields, hiking/walking, picnicking/grills, refreshments
* Douglas Park Greenway Trail *(New Broadway)*—picnicking
* Margotta Courts *(Valley St.)*
* Reverend Sykes Park *(Valley St.)*

SOMERS
* Reis Park *(Rte. 139)*

TARRYTOWN
* Glenville Woods *(Benedict Ave.)*—hiking/walking
* Patriot's Park *(next to the Warner Library)*—picnicking

TUCKAHOE
* Fisher Avenue Park *(Fisher Ave.)*
* Main Street Park *(Main St. & Marbledale Rd.)*
* Parkway Oval *(Consulate Dr.)*—fields
* Pleasant Place Park *(Pleasant Pl.)*

WHITE PLAINS
* Battle-Whitney Park *(Chatterton & Battle Aves.)*—fields
* Chatterton Playground *(Chatterton & Harmon Aves.)*
* Church Street School *(Church St.)*—swimming
* Delfino Park *(Lake St.)*—fields, picnicking/grills, refreshments, skating
* Druss Park (Bryant & Prospect Aves.)—picnicking
* Gardella Park *(Ferris & Park Aves.)*—fields, picnicking/grills, swimming, wading pool
* George Washington School *(Orchard St.)*—fields
* Gillie Park *(Mamaroneck Ave. & Gedney Way)*—fields
* Kittrell Park *(Bank St. & Fisher Ave.)* – swimming, wading pool
* Mamaroneck Avenue School *(Mamaroneck Ave.)*—fields
* Mattison Playground *(Quinby Ave. & Lynton Pl.)*—picnicking
* Mitchell Place Tot Lot *(Mitchell Pl.)*
* Old Tarrytown Road Park *(Old Tarrytown Rd.)*—picnicking/grills
* Post Road School *(Post Rd.)*—fields, swimming
* Ridgeway School *(Ridgeway Ave.)*—fields
* Slater Center *(Fisher Ct.)*
* Travis Hill Park *(Lincoln Ave.)*—fields, hiking/walking, picnicking/grills

11

* Turnure Park *(Main St.)*—picnicking/grills
* Washington Avenue Park *(Washington Ave.)*—picnicking/ grills
* Yosemite Park *(40 Yosemite Ave.)*—fields, picnicking/grills

YONKERS

* "Boo" Wilson Playground *(Tuckahoe Rd.)*
* Bregano Park & Playground *(Rigby St. & Brandon Rd.)*
* Bronx River Road Playground *(Bronx River Rd. & Winfred Ave.)*
* Buena Vista Playground *(107-109 Vista Ave.)*
* Caryl Avenue Playground *(Caryl & Saratoga Aves.)*
* Cedar Place Playground *(20 Cedar Pl.)*
* Cerone Avenue Playground *(Cerone Ave.)*
* Clemens Park & Playground *(Leighton Ave.)*
* Cochran Park & Playground *(Oliver Ave.)*
* Columbus Park & Playground *(Park Hill Ave.)*
* Coyne Park & Playground *(McLean & Old Jerome Aves.)*
* Culver Street Playground *(Culver St. & Livingston Ave.)*
* Doyle Park & Playground *(Walnut St. & Ashburton Ave.)*
* Dunn Park & Playground *(Glenwood & Vineyard Aves.)*
* Fay Park & Playground *(Abeel St.)*
* Ferme Park & Playground *(Brewster & Dunston Aves.)*
* Fleming Park & Playground *(Prescott St.)*
* Georgia Avenue Playground *(Georgia & Louisiana Aves.)*
* Gramatan Hills Playground *(Palmer Rd. & Little John Pl.)*
* Grant Park & Playground *(Park Ave.)*
* Irving Park & Playground *(View St. & Bartholdi Pl.)*
* Kinsley Park & Playground *(Park & Chase Aves.)*
* Lennon Park & Playground *(Lake & Park Aves.)*
* O'Boyle Park & Playground *(Hawthorne Ave.)*
* Pelton Park & Playground *(McLean & Van Cortlandt Park Aves.)*
* Pickett Park & Playground *(Knowles St. & Hawthorne Ave.)*
* Pitkin Park & Playground *(87 Locust Hill Ave.)*
* Post & Elliott Playground *(Post St. & Elliott Ave.)*
* Richter Park & Playground *(Nepperhan Ave. & Reade St.)*
* Ruebo-Cieslinski Park & Playground *(Edwards & Frederick Pls.)*
* Schultze Park & Playground *(St. Eleanoras Ln.)*
* Smith Park & Playground *(Nepperhan & Lake Aves.)*
* Stillwell Park & Playground *(1018 McLean Ave.)*
* Sullivan Oval Park & Playground *(Van Cortlandt Park Ave. & Spruce St.)*
* Tansey Park & Playground *(184 Stanley Ave.)*
* Trenchard Street Playground *(Trenchard St.)*

* Trevor Park & Playground *(Ravine Ave.)*
* Vark Street Park & Playground *(Vark St.)*
* Washington Park *(S. Broadway)*
* Welty Park & Playground *(Mile Square & Barton Rds.)*
* Wilson Park & Playground *(Alexander Ave.)*

YORKTOWN

* Blackberry Woods *(Marcy St., Shrub Oak)*
* Chelsea Park *(Gomer St., Yorktown Heights)* – fields
* Downing Park *(Rte. 202/Crompond Rd., near Rte. 132)*— fields, picnicking/grills
* George Washington Elementary School *(Lexington Ave., Mohegan Lake)*—fields
* Hanover East *(Wellington Rd., Yorktown Heights)*
* Ivy Knolls Park *(Ivy Rd. & Spring St., Shrub Oak)*—ice-skating
* Junior Lake Park *(Edgewater St., Yorktown Heights)* – ice-skating, picnicking/grills, swimming
* Lincoln Titus Elementary School *(Lincoln Ave., Crompond)*—fields
* Railroad Station Park *(Commerce St., Yorktown Heights)*
* Shrub Oak Park *(Sunnyside St., off of Rte. 6, Shrub Oak)*— fields, swimming
* Sparkle Lake *(Granite Springs Rd., Yorktown Heights)*— ice-skating, picnicking/grills, swimming beach
* Walden Woods *(Curry St., Yorktown Heights)*
* Willow Park *(Curry St., Yorktown Heights)*—fields, ice-skating
* York Hill Park *(Hawthorne Dr., Yorktown Heights)*—fields
* Yorktown Community and Cultural Center *(Commerce St., Yorktown Heights)*—fields

County & State Parks

The Westchester County Parks system alone covers more than 16,000 acres, and there are also two New York State Parks in the county. In addition to beautiful scenery, these places offer opportunities to hike, bike, swim, ice-skate, picnic and, in some cases, even play miniature golf.

Some of the county parks require a Park Pass for admission. Passes are available at many of the county park information centers, as well as at the Westchester County Center *(in White Plains)* and the Westchester County Parks Department *(in Mount Kisco)*. They cost $40 and are good for up to three years. Each pass allows free admission to county-owned park facilities for the pass holder and up to two guests; children under twelve are admitted for free. The pass also provides some discounts in user and parking fees. For more information, call the Parks Department at **(914) 864-PARK** or visit www.westchestergov.com/parks.

ARDSLEY
V.E. Macy Park
Saw Mill River Rd. (914) 946-8133

This centrally-located 172-acre park is a perfect spot for group picnics. There are bathroom facilities available.
Hours: Daily 8 am to dusk
Activities: Picnicking, playground
Admission: County Park Pass required

CORTLANDT
Croton Gorge Park
Rte. 129 (914) 827-9568

This ninety-seven-acre property at the base of the Croton Dam is a popular spot for fishing, picnicking and hiking, with direct trail access to New York State's Old Croton Aqueduct. The park is also available in winter for cross-country skiing and sledding. There are bathroom facilities.
Hours: Daily 8 am to dusk
Activities: Hiking/walking, nature study, picnicking, playground
Admission: Free

CROTON-ON-HUDSON
Croton Point Park
Croton Point Ave. (914) 862-5290

This 508-acre park offers year-round events and activities in addition to facilities for camping, hiking and swimming. The Croton Point Nature Center has a year-round schedule of interpretive programs. The beach is open on weekends and holidays. There are bathroom facilities and refreshments available.
Hours: Daily 8 am to dusk
Activities: Hiking/walking, nature study, picnicking, playground, swimming beach
Admission: Free

HARTSDALE
Ridge Road Park
Ridge Rd. (914) 946-8133

A 170-acre park offering picnicking facilities, ball fields and playgrounds. There are bathroom facilities.
Hours: Daily 8 am to dusk
Activities: Fields, nature study, picnicking, playground
Admission: County Park Pass required

MONTROSE
George's Island Park
Dutch St. (914) 737-7530

This 208-acre waterfront park contains tidal wetlands, a freshwater pond and wooded trails. It also provides boat access to the Hudson River and areas for nature study and picnicking. There are bathroom facilities.
Hours: Daily 8 am to dusk
Activities: Hiking/walking, nature study, picnicking, playground
Admission: Free

MOUNT VERNON
Willson's Woods Park
E. Lincoln Ave. (914) 813-6990

One of the oldest parks in the county, this twenty-three- acre park offers a beautiful swimming pool with an adjacent English Tudor-style bathhouse, as well as areas for picnicking and fishing. There are bathroom facilities and refreshments.
Hours: Daily 8 am to dusk
Activities: Hiking/walking, ice-skating, nature study, play ground, picnicking, swimming
Admission: County Park Pass required; Westchester residents only

NEW ROCHELLE
Glen Island Park
Pelham Rd. (914) 813-6720/-6721

Located on the Long Island Sound, this 105-acre park offers a variety of recreational facilities, including a beach, an eighteen-hole miniature golf course, a playground, a picnicking area with a pavilion, and magnificent waterfront views. There are bathroom facilities and refreshments available.
Hours: Daily 8 am to dusk
Activities: Hiking/walking, miniature golf, picnicking, play-ground, swimming beach
Admission: County Park Pass required; Westchester residents only

NORTH SALEM
Mountain Lakes Park
Hawley Rd. (914) 864-7310

Westchester's northernmost county park covers 1,038 acres and is characterized by a rugged landscape and a native hardwood forest with miles of trails. Located on the property is Mt. Bailey, the highest point in Westchester, which affords breathtaking vistas in every season. There are bathroom facilities.
Hours: Daily 8 am to dusk
Activities: Boat rentals, hiking/walking, ice-skating, nature study, swimming
Admission: Free

SLEEPY HOLLOW
Kingsland Point Park
Palmer Ave. (914) 631-1068

Home of the Historic Tarrytown Lighthouse, this eighteen-acre park has ball fields, picnic areas and kayaking. There are bathroom facilities.
Hours: Daily 8 am to dusk
Activities: Hiking/walking, nature study, playground
Admission: County Park Pass required

SOMERS
Lasdon Park, Arboretum & Veterans Memorial
Rte. 35 (914) 864-7268

This 234-acre property consists of a bird and nature sanctuary, woodlands, open grass meadows and formal gardens with flower and shrub specimens from all over the world. Lasdon is also the site of the Chinese Friendship Pavilion, a gift from the People's Republic of China to the citizens of Westchester. The park also houses four inspirational memorials and a museum honoring Westchester veterans. There are bathroom facilities.
Hours: Daily 8 am to dusk
Activities: Hiking/walking, nature study
Admission: Free

17

VALHALLA
Kensico Dam Plaza
Bronx River Parkway (914) 328-1542

At the base of the Kensico Dam, this property covers ninety-eight acres. The park hosts a wide variety of activities, including ethnic celebrations, concerts, antiques shows and arts and crafts shows. There are bathroom facilities and refreshments available.
Hours: Daily 8 am to dusk
Activities: Hiking/walking, nature study, picnicking, playground
Admission: Free

WHITE PLAINS
Saxon Woods Park
Mamaroneck Ave. (914) 995-4480

This 700-acre property offers a variety of recreational facilities, including a pool, picnic areas and an eighteen-hole miniature golf course. It also has the county's only playground that is accessible to the disabled. There are bathroom facilities and refreshments available.
Hours: Daily 8 am to dusk
Activities: Hiking/walking, miniature golf, nature study, picnicking, playground, swimming *(County Park Pass required for swimming)*
Admission: Free

YONKERS
Sprain Ridge Park
Jackson Ave. (914) 231-3450/-3452

Located on a ridge between the northbound and south-bound lanes of the Sprain Brook Parkway, this park's 278 acres include a developed portion with a pool complex and picnic areas. The remainder of the park is heavily wooded, with a variety of hiking and mountain bike trails. There are bathroom facilities and refreshments available.
Hours: Daily 8 am to dusk
Activities: Hiking/walking, nature study, picnicking, playground, swimming
Admission: County Park Pass required

Tibbetts Brook Park
Midland Ave. (914) 231-2865

One of the first parks developed by the County, this 161-acre park contains a 412' x 125' pool. The park offers many recreational activities throughout the year and hosts ethnic celebrations, fairs and festivals during the summer months. There are bathroom facilities and refreshments available.
Hours: Daily 8 am to dusk
Activities: Biking, hiking/walking, ice-skating, miniature golf, picnicking, playground, swimming
Admission: County Park Pass required; Westchester residents only

YORKTOWN HEIGHTS
Franklin D. Roosevelt State Park
2957 Crompond Rd. (914) 245-4434
www.nysparks.state.ny.us/parks

This park encompasses spacious picnic areas and a huge
pool that accommodates several thousand people at one
time. Fishing and boating are allowed in Mohansic Lake and
Crom Pond; rowboat rentals are also available in season.
There are bathroom facilities and refreshments available.
Hours: Daily 8 am to dusk; the pool is open in season,
weekdays 10 am–5 pm, weekends 10 am–6 pm.
Activities: Biking, boating, hiking/walking, ice-skating,
picnicking, playground, swimming
Admission: Free; parking, $5; pool use, $2 for adults and
$1 for children

NEW JERSEY
Van Saun County Park
216 Forest Ave., Paramus (201) 262-2627
www.co.bergen.nj.us/parks/Parks/Van%20Saun%20Park.htm

The park has several age-appropriate playgrounds—one
designed specifically for infants, one for toddlers, one for
young children and another for slightly older kids—as well
as a brand-new carousel and a little ride-on train that cir-
cles a small zoo. There is also a farmyard with chickens,
geese, sheep, goats, pigs and cows. In the summer months
there is a sprinkler spiral for children to run through. There
are picnic tables and refreshment are available.
Hours: Zoo—daily 10:30 am–4:30 pm, Weekends, April-
September 9:30 am–5 pm; carousel—daily 10 am–6 pm;
train—daily 10 am–5 pm
Activities: Biking, hiking/walking, picnicking, playground
Admission: Free; May–October, Fridays–Sundays and holidays—zoo admission is $2 per adult and $1 for children over
12; November–April, zoo admission is free
What to Know Before You Go: Like any family attraction,
this park is significantly more crowded on the weekends or
on a holiday, which can translate into long lines for the
zoo, the train ride or even the snack bar. If you find yourself there on a crowded day with an excited toddler, we

19

encourage the tag team approach: one parent gets in line while the other occupies the child. Be sure to bring a change of clothes as the sprinklers may prove too tempting to avoid. Simon once rode home in nothing but a diaper as everything else was soaked.

Savvy Suggestion

Strap on your helmets and head for the Bronx River Parkway for Bike, Skate & Scooter Sundays. The Parkway is closed to cars between North White Plains and Bronxville (a sixteen-mile stretch) from 10 am–2 pm every Sunday during May, June and September (except holiday weekends). Bike from the Westchester County Center south to Scarsdale Road in Yonkers. Skate or scooter from the Westchester County Center north to Fisher Lane in North White Plains.

Gardens & Other Gorgeous Places

In addition to playgrounds and parks, Westchester is home to a number of beautiful gardens. In the past, prominent residents—including celebrities, business tycoons and other notable somebodies—built mansions and castles that still dot the county, most with scenic gardens, fountains and beautiful Hudson River vistas. Some of these have become historic sites and museums, so you can pack your infant in a snuggly and catch up on some culture or begin teaching your older child about past aristocracy. And, of course, many of these are lovely places just for strolling and picnicking.

CROTON-ON-HUDSON
Van Cortlandt Manor
S. Riverside Ave. (914) 271-8981
www.hudsonvalley.org/web/vanc-main.html

The eighteenth-century stone manor house and reconstructed tenant house host cooking, spinning, weaving, brick manufacturing and blacksmithing demonstrations. The grounds include orchards as well as ornamental herb and heirloom vegetable gardens.
Hours: April–October, Wednesday–Monday 10 am–5 pm; November–December, weekends 10 am–4 pm; Closed January-March
Admission: House tours—$9 adults, $5 children 5–17, free for children under 5; grounds only—$4 per person

21

KATONAH
Caramoor Center for Music and the Arts
Rte. 137 (914) 232-5035
www.caramoor.org

You can tour this Mediterranean-style house museum or just enjoy strolling and picnicking in the magnificent gardens, which include a butterfly garden. On Thursdays and Fridays, May–December, afternoon tea is served at 3 pm. In addition to classical music and jazz performances, Caramoor also has concerts for children and families.
Hours: May–October, daily 10 am–5 pm; guided house tours are available Wednesday–Sunday, 1–4 pm
Admission: $7 adults, free for children under 17

NORTH SALEM
Hammond Museum & Japanese Stroll Garden
Deveau Rd. (914) 669-5033
www.hammondmuseum.org

Stroll through three acres of Japanese gardens, enjoy the
changing exhibits and eat in an outdoor café. The museum
also sponsors Saturday children's programs for ages 6–12,
including "Make a Bonsai Garden" and "Origami Mobile."
Hours: Wednesday–Sunday 12–4 pm; Sunday 11 am–3 pm
Admission: $5 adults, free for children under 12

PURCHASE
PepsiCo Sculpture Gardens
PepsiCo World Headquarters, Anderson Hill Rd.
(914) 253-2900

Also known as The Donald M. Kendall Sculpture Gardens,
this is a world-renowned garden and sculpture collection.
The collection contains some forty pieces of twentieth-
century art and features works by masters such as Auguste
Rodin and Alexander Calder. But more importantly for parents,
the 168 acres are open to the public, and there are walking
trails, flower gardens, picnic tables and a fish-stocked
pond. Maps for a free, self-guided tour—which will also
help you find your way around and distinguish which sculptures are which—are available at the information center.
There is a no-touch policy; nevertheless, this is a great
place to take children.
Hours: Daily 9 am–5 pm
Admission: Free
What To Know Before You Go: There is no café, so if you
plan to picnic, you need to bring food with you.

TARRYTOWN
Lyndhurst
635 S. Broadway (914) 631-4481
www.lyndhurst.org
This site has over sixty-five acres of manicured lawns, unusual
trees and shrubs, and winding paths. Highlights include The
Rose Garden, developed in the early 1990s, and great views
of the Hudson River and the Tappan Zee Bridge. The Carriage

House Café is open May–October, Wednesday–Sunday 11 am–3 pm.
Hours: April–October, Tuesday–Sunday and Memorial Day, Labor Day and Columbus Day 10 am–5 pm; November–April, weekends and Martin Luther King Day and Presidents' Day 10 am–4 pm
Admission: $10 adults, $4 ages 12-17, free for children under 12

Sunnyside
Sunnyside Ln., off Rte. 9 (914) 591-8763
www.hudsonvalley.org/web/sunn-main.html

The nineteenth-century home of author Washington Irving *("The Legend of Sleepy Hollow" and "Rip Van Winkle")* includes plantings, walkways and picnic grounds.
Hours: March, weekends 10 am–4 pm; April–October, Wednesday–Monday 10 am–5 pm; November–December, Wednesday–Monday 10 am–4 pm
Admission: House tours—$9 adults, $5 children 5–17, free for children under 5; grounds only—$4 per person

YONKERS
Untermyer Park and Gardens
945 N. Broadway (914) 377-6450

23

Developed in the early 1900s, this grand, Beaux Arts garden offers a Greek-style amphitheater, fountains, canals and Hudson River views.
Hours: Daily dawn to dusk
Admission: Free

MANHATTAN & THE BRONX
The Cloisters
Fort Tryon Park, Manhattan (212) 923-3700
www.metmuseum.org/hom.asp

Located on four acres overlooking the Hudson River in northern Manhattan, this branch of The Metropolitan Museum of Art is devoted to the art and architecture of medieval Europe. The building incorporates elements from medieval southern France, including cloisters and other monastic architecture. There are reproduction gardens, as well as approximately 5,000 works of medieval art such as tapestries and stained-glass windows. Gallery workshops for kids ages 4–12 and their families are held at held at 1 pm on the first Saturday of every month.

Hours: March–October, Tuesday–Sunday 9:30 am–5:15 pm; November–February, Tuesday–Sunday 9:30 am–4:45 pm; closed New Year's Day, Thanksgiving Day, Christmas Day

Admission: $12 adults, free for children under 12

What to Know Before You Go: The Trie Café serves breakfast, lunch and dessert May–October, Tuesday–Sunday, 10 am-4:30 pm. Free city parking is available in Fort Tryon Park. Strollers are not permitted on Sundays; back carriers are available for borrowing at the coat check.

New York Botanical Garden – Everett Children's Garden
Bronx River Parkway at Fordham Rd., Bronx (718) 817-8700
www.nybg.org/family/ecag.html

This twelve-acre indoor/outdoor science exploration center for kids features forty hands-on nature discovery activities, including mazes, galleries, microscopes, topiaries, treasure hunts, a sparkling waterfall and glorious gardens. The Garden also hosts Family Events, such as the Special Summer Storytelling Series, Scarecrow and Harvest Weekend, and Goodnight Garden and Goblin. Other programs, such as The Holiday Train Show *(a perennial favorite!)* and Garden Sprouts, a gardening program for kids ages 3–5 require additional fees.

Hours: April–June, weekdays 1–6 pm, weekends and Memorial Day 10 am–6 pm; July–August, Tuesday–Sunday 10 am–6 pm; September–October, weekdays 1–6 pm, weekends and holiday Mondays (Labor Day and Columbus Day) 10 am–6 pm; November–March, weekdays 1–4 pm, weekends and holiday Mondays *(Martin Luther King Day and Presidents' Day)* 10 am–4 pm

Admission: $3 adults, $1 children 2–12, free for children under 2 *(some exhibits require additional fees)*

What to Know Before You Go: Lunch and snacks are available in the Garden Café year-round. Picnic tables are located near the Everett Children's Adventure Garden, the Snuff Mill and the Snuff Mill River Terrace.

Wave Hill
675 W. 252nd St., Bronx (718) 549-3200
www.wavehill.org

Stroll through the various gardens, such as the wildflower
garden, herb garden or aquatic garden (*which has a small
pond filled with large goldfish*). Or just snag one of the
many Adirondack chairs and take in the spectacular public
garden overlooking the Hudson River. The drop-in "Family
Art Project" (*Kerlin Learning Center, Saturdays and Sundays
1–4 pm*) is free with admission to the grounds; your child
will learn to make paintings, prints, collages and sculptures
out of natural materials. There are also storytellers, singers,
dancers and musicians, as well as special events. The Wave
Hill Café serves light fare with outdoor seating Tuesday–Friday
11 am–4:30 pm; Saturday and Sunday 10 am–4:30 pm; Wednesdays
in June and July 10 am–8 pm. There is also a picnic area.
Hours: April 15–October 14, Tuesday–Sunday 9 am–5:30 pm;
open until 9 pm on Wednesdays in June and July. October
15–April 14, Tuesday–Sunday 9 am–4:30 pm. Open on
Memorial Day, Labor Day, Columbus Day; closed New Year's
Day, Martin Luther King Day, Presidents' Day, Thanksgiving,
Christmas Day.
Admission: March 15–November 14, free Tuesday all day
and Saturday 9 am–12 pm, Wednesday–Sunday, $4 adults,
free for children under 6; free November 15–March 14
What to Know Before You Go: There is a very small members-
only parking lot. You will probably have to park along the
road outside the gardens, so you may have a little hike
before you begin your leisurely stroll. For this reason, and
because the grounds are so vast, we suggest you bring a
stroller for toddlers who may get tired. But be aware that
some areas, like the aquatic garden, are only accessible by
steps, making strollers a somewhat cumbersome proposition.

PUTNAM COUNTY
Boscobel Restoration
Rte. 9D, Garrison (845) 265-3638
www.boscobel.org

The grounds of this historic house museum comprise a formal
rose garden with over 140 varieties of roses, fountains, an

apple orchard and an herb garden. The one-mile Woodland Trail winds through twenty-nine acres of wooded landscape and features vistas of the Hudson River, as well as a gazebo, bridge and benches. Christmas Candlelight Tours and other special events are held seasonally.

Hours: April-October, Wednesday–Monday 9:30 am–5 pm; November-December, Wednesday–Monday 9:30 am-4 pm; Closed January-March, Thanksgiving and Christmas

Admission: $10 adults, $7 children 6–14

Nature Centers & Preserves

If you or your child is into bird-watching, butterflies or reptiles, there are a lot of great places in Westchester to suit your needs. Filled with trails, these places are perfect for a leisurely stroll, a brisk outdoor walk, or a vigorous hike. While you're there, you can immerse yourself in nature study and help your child begin to learn to identify trees, plants and wildflowers. At the nature centers, kids can pet and hold live animals and take classes on nature, animals and crafts.

BEDFORD
Mianus River Gorge Preserve
167 Mianus River Rd. (914) 234-3455

Over 700 acres and five miles of walking trails along Westchester's only old growth forest.
Hours: April–November, daily 8:30 am–5 pm
Admission: Free

Westmoreland Sanctuary
260 Chestnut Ridge Rd. (914) 666-8448
www.westmorelandsanctuary.org

This 625-acre nature preserve has eight miles of trails, a museum and a variety of activities and educational programs. Activities for children include a Children's Nature Hike, Exploring Insects & Spiders, and an Annual Fall Festival with

a petting zoo, pony rides, arts and crafts projects, food and live animal presentations.
Hours: Trails—daily dawn to dusk; museum—Monday-Saturday 9 am–5 pm, Sunday 10:30 am–5 pm. Holiday schedules may vary.
Admission: Free

CHAPPAQUA
Pruyn Sanctuary Butterfly & Hummingbird Garden
275 Millwood Rd. (Rte. 133) (914) 666-6503

Over ninety acres with more than 125 types of annual and perennial flowering plants, over twenty-five species of butterflies and moths, and two dozen species of birds.
Hours: Daily dawn to dusk
Admission: Free

CROSS RIVER
Ward Pound Ridge Reservation
Rtes. 35 & 121 S. (914) 864-7317
www.westchestergov.com/parks/

Westchester County's largest park offers a variety of activities in all seasons, including a playground, miles of wooded trails, and areas for picnicking, fishing and cross-country skiing. The park is home to the Trailside Nature Museum, which hosts weekend nature programs year-round. There are bathroom facilities and refreshments available.
Hours: Daily 8 am to dusk
Admission: Free

CROTON-ON-HUDSON
Brinton Brook Nature Preserve
Albany Post Rd. (914) 666-6503

This is a wooded nature preserve with trails, a stream, a lake and ruins.
Hours: Daily dawn to dusk
Admission: Free

KATONAH
James Ramsey Hunt Sanctuary
N. Salem Rd., off Rte. 35 (914) 666-6177

Rich in birds and wildlife, this sanctuary covers over 200 acres of land. Its extensive trail system is complemented by a network of small bridges and boardwalks.
Hours: Daily dawn to dusk
Admission: Free

Marian Yarrow Nature Preserve
Mt. Holly Rd. (914) 244-3271

This preserve features extensive trails, a thirty-foot waterfall and Hidden Lake, a favorite watering hole for migratory birds.
Hours: Daily dawn to dusk
Admission: Free

MOUNT KISCO
Butler Sanctuary and Meyer Preserve
Chestnut Ridge Rd. (914) 244-3271

Boasting hundreds of acres of forest, streams, fields, scenic views and a well-marked trail system, this preserve is home to over 140 species of birds, 110 species of trees, shrubs and vines, and 250 species of wildflowers.
Hours: Daily dawn to dusk
Admission: Free

Marsh Sanctuary
114 South Bedford Rd. (914) 241-2808

This is a 120-acre sanctuary with a wildflower garden, a boardwalk for bird watching, a 350-seat Greek-style amphitheater, hiking trails and a boardwalk into the marsh.
Hours: Daily dawn to dusk
Admission: Free

NORTH WHITE PLAINS
Cranberry Lake Preserve
Old Orchard St. (914) 428-1005
www.westchester.gov/parks/NatureCenters/CranberryLake.htm

A nature preserve with 165 acres of forest, wetlands and a lake. Three miles of trails, including a loop around the lake, make for good strolling and hiking. The Nature Center offers interpretive programs every weekend throughout the year.
Hours: Trails—daily dawn to dusk; Nature Center—Tuesday–Saturday 9 am–4 pm
Admission: Free

OSSINING
Teatown Lake Reservation
1600 Spring Valley Rd. (914) 762-2912, ext.10
www.teatown.org

This 759-acre nature preserve and education center has over fourteen miles of walking and hiking trails; a Nature Center with live animals, including snakes, birds of prey, turtles, amphibians, rabbits and a porcupine; and a Nature Store with a broad selection of children's science materials, toys and nature-related books, as well as adult gifts, cards and stationery. The reservation also offers Environmental Education Programs for children and adults *(additional fees apply and pre-registration is required)*.
Hours: Nature Center—Tuesday–Saturday 9 am–5 pm, Sunday 1 pm–5 pm; Trails—dawn to dusk
Admission: Free
What to Know Before You Go: No bikes are allowed on the trails.

PEEKSKILL
Blue Mountain Reservation
Welcher Ave. (914) 862-5275
www.westchester.gov/parks

This 1,500-acre reservation features miles of trails for strolling and nature study as well as more challenging hikes to the tops of two large peaks, Mt. Spitzenberg and Blue

Mountain. There is a playground, as well as facilities for ice-skating and picnicking. There are bathroom facilities.
Hours: Daily 8 am to dusk
Admission: Free

RYE
Rye Nature Center
873 Boston Post Rd. (914) 967-5150
www.ci.rye.ny.us/nature.htm

This nature center has forty-seven acres of grounds, with two-and-a-half miles of nature trails. Trail maps are available outside the main building. The center offers a series of programs where kids ages 3–5 can explore the outdoors as well as participate in games, crafts, and songs. There is also a summer camp for kids ages 3 and up *(additional fees apply)*.
Hours: Grounds—daily 9 am–5 pm; Building—Monday-Saturday 10 am–4 pm
Admission: Free

SCARSDALE
Greenburgh Nature Center
99 Dromore Rd. (914) 723-3470
www.townlink.com/community_web/gnc

A thirty-three-acre woodland preserve that offers trails, a museum, a hands-on discovery room and live animals. There are seasonal programs, such as maple-sugaring, and the naturalist staff leads classes and programs, like "Nature Bugs and Critters" and "Crafts & Kids," that involve nature discovery for kids ages 3–5 with a parent or caregiver. No need to sign up: you can take these classes on an ad hoc basis *(additional fees apply)*.
Hours: Grounds—daily dawn to dusk; Manor House—Saturday–Thursday 9:30 am–4:30 pm; Animal Museum *(inside the Manor House)*— weekdays 9:30 am–noon and 1–4:30 pm, weekends 10 am–4:30 pm
Admission: Free admission to the grounds; Manor House—$4 adults, $2 children 2–12; Greenburgh residents with Unicard pay half-price; members enter for free

What to Know Before You Go: The trails are unpaved and can be bumpy. Watch running toddlers, and if you use a stroller make sure it has big tires.

Weinberg Nature Center
455 Mamaroneck Rd. (914) 722-1289
www.scarsdale.com/weinberg.asp

A ten-acre sanctuary with live animals, a meadow, a fruit orchard, an apiary for bees, and a butterfly and humming-bird garden. Stroll the trails, visit the Trailside Nature Museum for nature-related exhibits, meditate in the Japanese-style Zen Garden and lunch in the picnic area. A Native American Village explores the history of the Lenape and Iroquois Tribes. Special events and programs for toddlers include hands-on sensory awareness, exploration and discovery sessions, storybook time and live animals *(additional fees apply)*.
Hours: Grounds—dawn to dusk; Interpretive Center—September-June, Wednesday–Sunday 9 am–5 pm; July-August, Monday–Friday 9 am–5 pm
Admission: Voluntary donation

31

TARRYTOWN
Rockefeller State Park Preserve
Rte. 117, 1 mile east of Rte. 9 *(Between Sleepy Hollow & Pleasantville)* (914) 631-1470
www.nysparks.state.ny.us/parks

This park has a wide variety of habitats, including wetlands, woodlands, meadows, fields and a lake. Carriage paths that traverse the park are ideal for strolling and jogging. The Visitor Center hosts exhibits of local and historical interest. There are bathroom facilities.
Hours: Daily 8 am to dusk
Admission: Free; parking is $5 *(April–October, Wednesday–Sunday 9 am–4:30 pm; November–March, weekends & holidays only)*

AND DON'T FORGET...
Bronx River Parkway Reservation
Yonkers to Valhalla (914) 723-4058

Westchester's oldest park, this 807-acre, paved "linear park" was created as an adjunct to the Bronx River Parkway, which opened in 1925. The reservation features miles of paths for biking, walking, and nature study, as well as ponds, wooden footbridges and hundreds of varieties of native trees and shrubs.
Hours: Daily 8 am to dusk
Admission: Free

Other Outdoor Attractions

These three spots need a category of their own. For an older child, or an active younger one, these attractions will keep your family busy all day long.

FISHKILL
Splash Down Water Park/Adventure Island
2200 Rte. 9 (845) 896-6606
www.splashdownpark.com

Splash Down features three large water slides, a pirate ship with five kiddie slides, a large activity pool, a water spray area and a water balloon game. If you don't feel like getting wet, there is miniature golf, mini basketball, and a large picnic area. Adventure Island has a soft play area with tunnels, tubes, chutes and a ball pit, in addition to a giant slide, bumper cars, bumper boats, miniature golf and many games.
Hours: Memorial Day Weekend–Labor Day Weekend, daily 10 am–7 pm
Admission: Splash Down—$9.50–$16.95 (*depending on height*), $5.50 for spectators; with Adventure Island—$9.50–$22.95 (depending on height); free for infants
What to Know Before You Go: Coolers are allowed for picnicking but glass containers and alcoholic beverages are not allowed. Swim attire should not have any rivets, buckles or metal.

JEFFERSON VALLEY
Osceola Beach & Picnic Grounds
399 E. Main St. (914) 245-3246
www.osceolabeach.com

In addition to a beach, this destination spot on Lake Osceola features miniature golf, bumper boats, paddle boats, kayaks, pony rides, a kiddie play park with an air castle, and people dressed up as cartoon characters and clowns. You can buy food from the snack bar, bring your own lunch or cook on their grills.

Hours: Weekdays 9:30 am–6 pm; weekends and holidays 8 am–6 pm; swimming—daily (weather permitting) 10 am–6 pm
Admission: Weekdays, $5 adults, $4 children; weekends and holidays, $10 adults, $6 children; free for children 3 and under. Price includes parking, admission and beach access. Additional fees apply for miniature golf, pony rides, boating and some other activities.

RYE
Playland
Playland Parkway (914) 813-7000
www.ryeplayland.org

33

This amusement park offers over fifty rides for children and adults, including roller coasters, vertical thrills and water rides. Kiddyland has rides for kids ages two and over. Playland also has a swimming pool, lake boating and kayaking, mini golf, indoor ice-skating, a picnic area, free entertainment, arcade games, and a beach, boardwalk and pier on Long Island Sound. You'll find traditional amusement park foods and snacks, such as pizza, cotton candy, etc., as well as chains such as Burger King, Nathan's, Carvel and Captain Hook's seafood restaurant.

Hours: Hours vary, depending on season, activity and weather— call or check the website for details.
Admission: Tickets cost $1.25 (the per-ticket price is lower if you buy multi-ticket books) and rides cost 2–4 tickets each. Parking is $5 on weekdays, $7 on weekends and $10 on holidays.
What to Know Before You Go: Some Kiddyland rides have height restrictions and many do not allow adults to ride with the children. Use caution when visiting with the weekend mobs—keep an eye on your child at all times.

Savvy Suggestions

Summer Fun
* Invite the neighborhood kids over to run in the sprinkler
* Saxon Woods Park for miniature golf, playground and swimming
* Hudson Valley Shakespeare Festival at Boscobel
* Van Saun County Park—there's something here for everyone!
* Animals and hayrides at Muscoot Farm
* Organize a small picnic at a local playground or park
* Feed the animals in The Children's Zoo at The Bronx Zoo

The Great Indoors

Indoor Play
Libraries
Bookstores with Story Times
Arts & Crafts Walk-Ins

When it's too hot (or too cold) to go to your neighborhood playground, rest assured that there is an abundance of indoor activities to keep you and your child amused and engaged for hours. From exploring climbing equipment at an indoor play space to exploring every book about fire trucks ever written (*both Sam's and Simon's favorites*), there are many spots that will keep you and your child busy and happy. One point to keep in mind: if you decided that one of these activities would be the perfect thing to do on rainy day, chances are so did lots and lots of other parents. Our advice— particularly for play spaces, shopping centers and walk-in facilities—is to go when they open. It'll get more crowded as the day goes on, but you can get in a good hour or two of fun before it gets uglier than a one-day clearance sale at Loehmann's.

Savvy Suggestion

Keep a container filled with pennies in your car for when you need an impromptu activity. Head to The Westchester and let your child toss pennies into the fountain while "making a wish."

35

Indoor Play

Not long after the little creatures begin walking do you find yourself desperately searching for places they can go running. Luckily, there are many indoor play spaces in and around Westchester. Most are well-equipped with climbing structures, sandboxes, ride-on toys, train sets and more.

Savvy Suggestion

Make Your Own Play-dough

2 cups flour	2 cups boiling water
1 cup salt	2 tbsp. oil
4 tsp. cream of tartar	food coloring

Mix dry ingredients together. Add coloring to boiling water. Combine everything together. Stir until dough pulls away from bowl. Knead until smooth. Store in fridge.

Generally, there is an admission fee for the kids, but grown-ups enter for free. Before celebrating what a good deal that is, remember, it's a deal with the devil. When they're climbing up the habitrail-for-humans, so are you. When they're sprinting through the 10,000 square feet of floor space, so are you. Some parents get away with blithely reading a magazine or chatting with friends while their little ones try to disprove the laws of gravity, but most parents are keeping a close eye on their kids. This is a great way to spend a morning or an afternoon when you don't want to be outside. Remember, weekends and inclement weather can make indoor play spaces a bit of a mob scene, but if you and your child can handle it, God bless.

ELMSFORD
Sportime USA
380 Saw Mill River Rd., *(Rt. 9A)* # 1 (914) 592-2111
www.sportime-usa.com

Over 40,000 square feet of indoor sports and amusements,
including over 200 video/arcade games, sports activities,
wall climbing, laser tag, billiards, batting cages, bowling,
bumper cars and more.
Hours: Sunday–Thursday 11 am–10:30 pm, Friday 11 am–
12:30 am, Saturday 10 am–12:30 am
Cost: Varies, depending on activity
Ages: 3 and up

MOUNT KISCO
Playscape
195 N. Bedford Rd. *(Manufacturer's Outlet Center)*
(914) 242-5321

Playscape is 10,000 square feet of pure fun. It's bright, clean
*(well, as clean as any place filled with dozens of children
can be)* and extremely well-equipped. With a massive indoor
sandbox, a pirate ship, slides, a "fun tower," blocks, dress-up
areas, a mini-basketball court, ride-on toys, and basic refreshment bar with seating, this place has it all.
Hours: Monday–Saturday 10 am–6 pm, Sunday 11 am–6 pm
Admission: $8 first child, $6 siblings
Ages: 7 and under
What to Know Before You Go: Although Playscape is
always open for general play, up to three birthday parties
can be going on at the same time, so call ahead to see how
crazy it is before hitting the road. While the Mount Kisco
outlet center is no Woodbury Commons, it does have a few
decent stores, including a Carter's outlet. After the kids
have burned off all their energy, they may not mind if you
take a quick spin through the stores.

NEW ROCHELLE
New Roc City
New Roc City, 33 Lecount Pl. *(Exit 16 off I-95)*
(914) 637-7575
www.newroccity.com

New Roc City comprises several facilities. The Fun House is
a play center for all ages. With four acres under one roof,
there are rides, multi-sensory entertainment, laser tag,
bumper cars, a thirty-foot climbing wall and arcade games.
New Roc Ice is a regulation-sized ice-skating rink. New Roc
'n Bowl has forty-eight fully computerized automatic bowling lanes with bumpers that go up and down so parents and
children can play together, as well as lightweight balls and
ramps to make it a fun and easy experience for children as
young as three. Regal Cinemas has eighteen movie theaters,
including an IMAX theater. Not surprisingly there are several
kid-friendly restaurants in the New Roc City complex,
including Applebee's and Zanaro's.
Hours: Opens daily at 10 am; call individual businesses
for closing times.
Cost: Varies, depending on activity
Ages: All ages

PORT CHESTER
Leapin' Lizards
421 Boston Post Rd., 3rd floor *(Kohl's Shopping Center)*
(914) 937-JUMP
www.leaplizards.com

Climb, bounce, crawl, jump and slide through tunnels,
mazes, slides, ball baths, foam forests, obstacle courses and
more. There is also a game room with arcade games and
toddler rides. There's a lot of climbing, so if your kids are
not strong climbers you may want to hold off until they
get more comfortable. Once they enter the maze of tubes
and tunnels you may find yourself crawling in behind them
if they get lost. There are several value-packs and member-
ships that will save you money if you plan to go frequently.
Hours: Daily 10 am–4 pm
Admission: $7.99, $6.99 on weekdays before 3 pm for
children under 5
Ages: 1–12

What to Know Before You Go: There is a snack bar with seating available at a central location, so you can keep an eye on your kids. You cannot bring meals from the outside, but they do have standard "kid's fare" if you want to feed your kids there.

TUCKAHOE
Locomotion
95 Lake Ave. (914) 337-4722

Probably the smallest of the indoor play spaces, this is great for less active toddlers. They have toys, trains, a dress-up area, some ride-on or push toys and a large sandbox as well as a climbing structure. Locomotion is also accessible by train *(Metro North's Harlem line, across from the Tuckahoe Station),* so it's perfect for non-driving babysitters.
Hours: Varies depending on classes and party schedules, but general schedule is: Monday, Tuesday, Thursday and Friday 10 am–5 pm, Wednesday 11 am–5 pm, Saturday 11 am–6 pm, Sunday 12–6 pm
Admission: $10 for 4 hours
Ages: 1–5
What to Know Before You Go: Call ahead to make sure it is open for general play as it is sometimes closed for private birthday parties or classes, especially on the weekends. Locomotion does not allow food or drink in the play room and only sells a few snacks. There is a pizzeria next door if you want to grab a slice before or after your outing.

WHITE PLAINS
Frozen Ropes
55 S. Broadway (914) 993-6355
www.frozenropes.com

This is part of a national chain of baseball and softball training facilities. They have indoor batting cages and pitcher's mounds.
Hours: Weekdays 3–9 pm, weekends 10 am–6 pm
Cost: $20 per 15 minutes
Ages: 6 and up

YONKERS
Kid-o-Robics
Cross County Shopping Center *(Upper Mall, near Macy's)*
(914) 965-2000

This play space boasts one of the largest soft play areas around, including five ball pits, a zipline, a trapeze and two giant slides. They also have an arcade with over thirty ticket-redemption games and rides. Some admission packages include a meal pass *(a slice of pizza, small popcorn and small soda)*. Or, when they're ready, your kids can go from the ball pit to a pit stop at the snack bar, which has a few other kid-friendly offerings.
Hours: Monday–Thursday 9 am–8 pm, Friday–Saturday 9 am–9 pm, Sunday 10 am–8 pm
Admission: $5–11 per child, depending on admission package and time
Ages: All ages
What to Know Before You Go: Since there is really just one big play area, younger, tentative children may be intimidated by the running and jumping "big kids." Because Kid-o-Robics is located in the massive Cross County Shopping Center, there are tons of stores, casual restaurants, several department stores and a movie theater nearby.

PUTNAM COUNTY
PlayZone
1511 Rte. 22, Suite C-21 *(Lake View Shopping Plaza)*, Brewster
(845) 279-5378

There's something for everyone here at this play space designed with physical and creative development in mind. There are three age-appropriate play structures (which is a great feature for those of us whose toddler has been pummeled by a pack of rambunctious first-graders exploding through a climbing tube!), a basketball area, an extra-large sandbox, a game room and a car track, as well as floor activities like Legos, blocks and a train table.
Hours: Monday–Saturday 10 am–6 pm, Sunday 11 am–6 pm
Admission: $8 first child, $6 siblings
Ages: 1–8

CONNECTICUT
Adventure Kids
16 Old Track Rd., Greenwich (*Exit 3 off I-95*)
(203) 861-2227
www.adventurekids.com

Kids can climb and slide through soft play mazes designed for even the youngest explorers. There is a toddler area set up exclusively for the little ones that includes a padded ball pit. Enjoy videos and wildlife and ecology demonstrations in the "Adventure Area" amphitheater. While the younger children romp through the mazes, the older kids can enjoy themselves in the arcade.
Hours: Daily 10 am–5 pm
Admission: $9.35 children 1 and up *(price includes 4 tokens for arcade play)*, $5.75 children under 1
Ages: 0-12
What to Know Before You Go: It's located very close to the Bruce Museum *(see listing in Chapter 5)*, which also has its own playground. Weather permitting, you can make it a fun indoor and outdoor daytrip. Adventure Kids is also only a few minutes from Main Street in Greenwich, which is packed with stores, restaurants and specialty shops.

41

ROCKLAND COUNTY
Jeepers
The Palisades Center, West Nyack (*exit 12 off I 287*), on the thEATery level (845) 353-5700
www.jeepers.com

This is an indoor family amusement park with rides geared to all different age groups (ranging from kiddie rides to an indoor roller coaster), games, soft play areas with tubes, chutes, slides and obstacle courses, and a specially-designed play area for toddlers and preschoolers.
Hours: Monday–Thursday 11 am–9 pm, Friday 11 am–10 pm, Saturday 10 am–10 pm, Sunday 11 am–8 pm
Admission: $6.99 children under 3 feet, $12.99 children over 3 feet *(games require additional fees)*
Ages: 2–12

Savvy Suggestions

Stay-at-Home Activities

* Thread Cheerios on string for an edible necklace *(mini pretzels work too)*.
* Cook something fun—whether it's baking cookies or English muffin pizza-faces.
* Keep discarded "trash" items like cardboard toilet paper rolls and empty boxes—you can use them for crafts.
* Practice measuring, pouring, counting and sorting with dried beans and pasta.
* Tape butcher paper on the floor and/or walls and let your child draw and paint the room.
* Keep some extra games, toys or arts and crafts materials in your "gift closet" just in case you get snowed in and need something new and different to play with.

Libraries

The only thing better than keeping your child entertained is doing it for free. The local libraries in Westchester offer a wide range of story hours and events for the little ones—including Story Times, Music, Arts & Crafts, and more—primarily for ages 6 months and up. For some programs, you must be a resident of that town or village, and certain programs may require advance registration. Usually all you'll need is a library card to attend. Many of the libraries also have wonderful Children's Rooms that are great places to just hang out. The librarians are incredibly helpful and don't mind putting away the stacks of books you and your child discovered on your visit.

Seriously, this is the best bargain going in Westchester. In addition to books, you can check out videos and DVDs (for you or your children), which you get to keep for a week—imagine what that would cost at Blockbuster. Libraries also lend out CDs and most have high-speed internet access. Each library posts its own hours, which may change from summer to winter. For information on the Westchester Library System, as well as on individual libraries, go to **www.westchesterlibraries.org**.

ARDSLEY
9 American Legion Dr. (914) 693-6636

ARMONK
19 Whippoorwill Rd. East (914) 273-3887

ARMONK/NORTH WHITE PLAINS BRANCH
10 Clove Rd. (914) 948-6359

BEDFORD
On the Village Green (914) 234-3570

BEDFORD HILLS
26 Main St. (914) 666-6472

BRIARCLIFF MANOR
Library Rd. (914) 941-7072

BRONXVILLE
201 Pondfield Rd. (914) 337-7680

CHAPPAQUA
195 S. Greeley Ave. (914) 238-4779

CROTON-ON-HUDSON
171 Cleveland Dr. (914) 271-6612

DOBBS FERRY
55 Main St. (914) 693-6614

EASTCHESTER
11 Oak Ridge Pl. (914) 793-5055

GREENBURGH
300 Tarrytown Rd. (914) 993-1600

43

HARRISON
Downtown *(Main)* Library
Bruce Ave. (914) 835-0324

Harrison/West Harrison Branch
2 Madison St. (914) 948-2092

HASTINGS-ON-HUDSON
Maple Ave. (914) 478-3307

IRVINGTON
12 S. Astor St. (914) 591-7840

KATONAH
26 Bedford Rd. (914) 232-3508

LARCHMONT
121 Larchmont Ave. (914) 834-2281

MAMARONECK
136 Prospect Ave. (914) 698-1250

MONTROSE
Hendrick Hudson Free Library
185 Kings Ferry Rd. (914) 739-5654

MOUNT KISCO
100 Main St. (914) 666-8041

MOUNT VERNON
28 S. First Ave. (914) 668-1840

NEW ROCHELLE
1 Library Plaza (914) 632-7878

Huguenot Children's Library
794 North Ave. (914) 632-8954

NORTH SALEM
276 Titicus Road/Rte. 116 (914) 669-5161

OSSINING
53 Croton Ave. (914) 941-2416

PEEKSKILL
Field Library
4 Nelson Ave. (914) 737-1212

PELHAM
530 Colonial Ave. (914) 738-1234

PLEASANTVILLE
Mount Pleasant Public Library
350 Bedford Rd. (914) 769-0548

Valhalla Branch
125 Lozza Dr. (914) 741-0276

PORT CHESTER
1 Haseco Ave. (914) 939-6710

POUND RIDGE
The Hiram Halle Memorial Library
271 Westchester Ave. (914) 764-5085

PURCHASE
3093 Purchase St. (914) 948-0550

RYE
1061 Boston Post Rd. (914) 967-0480

SCARSDALE
54 Olmsted Rd. (914) 722-1300

SOMERS
Rte. 139/Reis Park (914) 232-5717

SOUTH SALEM
15 Main St. (914) 763-3857

TARRYTOWN
The Warner Library
121 North Broadway (914) 631-7734

TUCKAHOE
71 Columbus Ave. (914) 961-2121

WHITE PLAINS
100 Martine Ave. (914) 422-1476

YONKERS
Crestwood Branch
16 Thompson St. (914) 337-1500

Grinton I. Will Branch
1500 Central Park Ave. (914) 337-1500

Riverview Branch
1 Larkin Ctr, (914) 337-1500

YORKTOWN/SHRUB OAK
John C. Hart Memorial Library
1130 Main St. (914) 245-5262

Savvy Suggestion

"Test drive" books or videos from the library on your kids before buying your own copies.

Bookstores with Story Times

Not to be overlooked, many bookstores *(including Barnes & Noble and Borders Books)* hold free story times and other special events for children. These can include author readings, costume character story times and children's performers, just to name a few. While you're certainly never obligated to buy anything, once they've got you there they know there's a decent chance that you'll buy a few of the titles you and your child have been reading. After all, children make very persuasive salespeople, do they not? Most of the big bookstores also have cafés or coffee shops, so you can grab a much-needed jolt of caffeine after thirty-seven consecutive recitations of *The Very Hungry Caterpillar*. Check their websites or stop by one of the locations listed below to find out about upcoming events. While these major bookstore chains seem to have stores on every corner, the ones listed below have children's programming.

HARTSDALE
Barnes & Noble
111 S. Central Ave. (914) 948-1002
www.barnesandnoble.com

MOUNT KISCO
Borders Books
162 E. Main St. (914) 241-8387
www.bordersstores.com

SCARSDALE
Borders Books
680 White Plains Rd. (914) 725-4637
www.bordersstores.com

WHITE PLAINS
Borders Books
West Chester Pavilion (914) 421-1110
www.bordersstores.com

YONKERS
Barnes & Noble
2614 Central Park Ave. (914) 771-6400
www.barnesandnoble.com

Arts & Crafts Walk-Ins

On a rainy afternoon your child may not be able to run wild, but at least his imagination can. Check out one of the local arts & crafts studios, where kids can take part in a variety of fun projects, from ceramic painting to sand art. Some places charge an hourly fee and some charge a project fee, and there is typically a wide range of projects and prices. What grandparent, teacher or other special person in your child's life wouldn't love a hand-made keepsake to proudly display?

DOBBS FERRY
Art In Us
145 Palisade St. (914) 591-5377
www.artinusonline.com

Saturday drop-offs for ages 3–6. Different projects.
Hours: Saturdays 11:30 am–1:30 pm
Cost: $15 per hour

LARCHMONT
Children's Creative Corner
7 Addison St. (914) 833-2880

Forty-five different projects for ages 2–14.
Hours: Weekdays 10 am–5:30 pm, weekends 10 am–7 pm
Cost: $12 per hour

Paint Your Art Out
2005 Palmer Ave. (914) 833-2321
www.paintyourartout.com

Ceramic painting.
Hours: During the school year—Tuesday, Wednesday and Saturday 11 am–6 pm, Thursday 11 am–8 pm, Friday 1:30–8 pm, Sunday 12–5 pm; summer hours—Wednesday and Saturday 11 am–6 pm, Thursday and Friday 11 am–9 pm
Cost: $7–66, depending on the piece *(includes firing fee)*

MAMARONECK
Come Out and Clay
253 Mamaroneck Ave. (914) 777-3761

Ceramic painting and mosaics.
Hours: Tuesday–Wednesday 11 am–7 pm, Thursday–Friday 11 am–9 pm, Saturday 11 am–8 pm, Sunday noon–7 pm
Cost: Per hour, $6 children, $8 adults, plus cost of piece ($5–60); there are also some specials, such as Two-for-Tuesdays, when two people are admitted for the price of one.

MOHEGAN LAKE
Let's Be Creative
1950 E. Main St. (914) 528-7888

Ceramic painting.
Hours: Tuesday–Sunday 12–5 pm
Cost: $11–200, depending on the piece *(includes 1½ hours of studio time, glazing and firing)*

SCARSDALE
Fun Craft
590 Central Park Ave. (914) 472-1748

Ceramic painting and sand art.
Hours: Daily 10 am–6 pm
Cost: $9–11, depending on the piece

Savvy Suggestions

Getting Out of the House on a Rainy Day

* Go to a toy store and let your child play—there are often train sets and other toys set up for demonstration purposes.
* Play with snakes at the Greenburgh Nature Center.
* Visit your local library to read, play on the computer, and meet other families.
* Go to Barnes & Noble or Borders, read books, and treat your child to a hot cocoa.
* Go to the pet store and look at the animals.

The People in Your Neighborhood

Community Centers

When it comes to finding the activities and support you need, community centers should be some of the first places you look. They are great places to find parenting workshops, programs for toddlers and children (including nursery school, child care and school holiday programs) and classes for your child and for you. At these centers, you'll find programs such as Mommy & Me, Gymnastics, Play, Music, Arts & Crafts, Dance, Martial Arts, Swimming and Foreign Language classes. Some of these facilities have playgrounds, some have children's theaters and some have pools where you can go for free swim. Many also have fitness centers, so you can exercise while your little one enjoys one of the dozens of activities offered. Another advantage to these all-in-one facilities is that you will find community-centered programs or support groups where you can meet other parents and families and take part in the many other adult programs.

At some centers you'll have to join in order to sign up for classes and workshops. At others you won't have to be a member, but there's usually a discount if you are. Membership fees vary, so call the center nearest you to find out the cost. For finding community centers, these websites are most helpful: **www.ymca.net, www.ywca.org** and **www.jcca.org**.

MOUNT KISCO
Boys & Girls Club of Northern Westchester
351 Main St. (914) 666-8069
www.boysandgirlsclubnw.org

MOUNT VERNON
Mount Vernon Family Center/YMCA
20 S. 2nd Ave., (914) 668-4041

YM-YWHA of Southern Westchester
30 Oakley Ave. (914) 664-0500

NEW ROCHELLE
New Rochelle YMCA
50 Weyman Ave. (914) 632-1818

PLEASANTVILLE
Richard G. Rosenthal JCC of Northern Westchester
600 Bear Ridge Rd. (914) 741-0333
www.rosenthaly.org

PORT CHESTER
Port Chester/Rye Brook Family Center/YMCA
400 Westchester Ave. (914) 939-7800

RYE
YMCA of Rye
21 Locust Ave. (914) 967-6363
www.ryeymca.org

SCARSDALE
JCC of Mid-Westchester
999 Wilmot Rd. (914) 472-3300
www.mwjcc.org/jccmidwestchester.htm

TARRYTOWN
Family YMCA at Tarrytown
62 Main St. (914) 631-4807
www.ymcatarrytown.org

JCC on the Hudson
371 S. Broadway (914) 366-7898
www.jcconthehudson.org

WHITE PLAINS
YMCA of Central & Northern Westchester
250 Mamaroneck Ave. (914) 949-8030

YWCA of White Plains and Central Westchester *(North Street Y)*
515 North St. (914) 949-6227
www.ywcawhiteplains.com

YONKERS
YMCA of Yonkers
17 Riverdale Ave. (914) 963-0183

YWCA of Yonkers
87 S. Broadway (914) 963-0640
www.ywcayonkers.org

MANHATTAN AND THE BRONX
92nd Street Y
1395 Lexington Ave., New York (212) 996-1100
www.92ndsty.org

Riverdale YM-YWHA
5625 Arlington Ave., Bronx
(718) 548-8200
www.RiverdaleY.org

CONNECTICUT
Greenwich Family YMCA
50 E. Putnam Ave., Greenwich
(203) 869-1630
www.gwymca.org

ROCKLAND COUNTY
Rockland County YMCA
35 S. Broadway, Nyack (845) 358-0245
www.rocklandymca.org

Rockland YM-YWHA
900 Rte. 45, Suite 15, New City (914) 362-4400
www.jccyofrockland.org

53

Savvy Suggestion

Here's a cheap thrill. Go to your local fire station. The fireman will happily show you around, and often will let children sit in the fire trucks and see the flashing lights. Many stations give kids a plastic fireman's helmet to take home so they'll never forget their visit.

Class Acts

Mommy & Me
Gymnastics & Play
Music
Arts & Crafts
Dance
Martial Arts
Swimming
Foreign Language

Enrolling your child in a class is a fun way to provide some structure to her day, and it will give you something entertaining to do as well. In addition to teaching your child new skills, classes also provide a setting in which she can learn to socialize and engage with other children and in which you can meet other parents and make friends. We both came out of classes with long-lasting friendships for Simon, Sam and ourselves.

When your child is quite young, you'll probably be enrolling more for you than for him—Laura enrolled Sam in Gymboree at six weeks to get out of the house and meet other parents. Later, you'll want to match your choices to your child—if she's a regular Mexican jumping bean, a gymnastics class might be a better choice than a sit-still arts & crafts program.

There's no shortage of classes in the Westchester area, so once you've decided what kind to take it's really a matter of finding one that works for your child's schedule. When enrolling younger children, be forewarned: the minute you sign up for a class that works perfectly for Junior's routine and plunk down a check, his nap time is guaranteed to change. Maybe it's just Murphy's Law, but it's true. Anyway, it's best not to second-guess when you think his nap time will be; most often the programs are flexible enough to let you switch from one time or day to another. Other considerations in selecting a class include location, class size and program structure and philosophy. And, since the success of the class is largely dependent on the specific teacher, ask around for recommendations. If you find teachers you like, stick with them.

In addition to the classes listed here, check your local community center (*listed in Chapter 3*)—most offer a variety of classes for kids. One final note: most places that offer classes also host birthday parties, so if your son loves his weekly music class, he may be thrilled to share it with his friends.

Mommy & Me

For many parents, adjusting to the new "bundle of joy" is a process that extends far beyond sleep deprivation and trying to find a single piece of clothing that doesn't have some sort of baby-induced stain on it. Signing up for a Mommy & Me program (*which often can include daddies and caregivers, too*) can be a great way to connect with other moms, share your experiences and get advice from a child development specialist. Most programs consist of playtime for parents and kids together, followed by a discussion led by a facilitator while the kids are watched by baby-sitters. Classes are usually grouped by children's ages, so the issues you are dealing with will be similar to the other mothers' concerns. Mommy & Me programs for older children are often aimed at laying the groundwork for parent/child separation. This may mean children are in one room doing arts and crafts or having a snack while moms are in a room across the hall—close enough if separation anxiety sets in, regardless of whether it's your child's or your own!

In addition to the classes listed below, check with your local religious institutions, as they often have these types of programs.

MOUNT KISCO
The Parent Center
104 Main St. (914) 378-5007

Hosted by Mount Kisco Recreation, the center offers cooperative playgroups for children from newborn to 4 years. Children participate in a variety of activities, including arts and crafts. A special group is offered for first-time parents with children under 9 months.

WHITE PLAINS
Parent's Place
3 Carhart Ave. (914) 948-5187

Established in 1976, Parent's Place strives to increase a parent's knowledge and confidence in a supportive environment while allowing infants and preschoolers to play and explore in a stimulating and fun setting. The skilled staff is made up of social workers and early childhood educators. This is a drop-in facility, meaning no registration is necessary; you may come as often or infrequently as you like. **Hours:** Mondays, Thursdays and Fridays 10 am to noon, Tuesdays 10 am to noon (*ages 2 and under*), Tuesdays 1:15–2:45 pm (*ages 9 months and under*)

ROCKLAND COUNTY
Rockland Parent-Child Center
137 1st Ave., Nyack (845) 358-2702

Free support groups for parents of infants (*ages 12 months and younger*) and toddlers (*ages 1-3*). Sessions include a discussion led by a social worker or facilitator. One evening a week there is also a support group for single parents.

CONNECTICUT
Just Wee Two
449 Pemberwick Rd., Greenwich (*Western Greenwich Civic Center*)
31 Cascade Rd., Stamford (*North Stamford Congregational Church*)
(800) 404-2204
www.justweetwo.com
Programs for children ages 14 months to 3½ years, taught

by early childhood teachers. Children are encouraged to explore, discover and interact through activities such as music, arts & crafts, playtime and stories. There are partial separation, preschool readiness and total separation programs.

Savvy Suggestions

New Parents

* Join a baby group: you'll find signs on bulletin boards in pediatrician's offices and grocery stores—connecting with other moms is really important.
* Keep your diaper bag packed. Refill it when you get home, so it's ready to go next time.
* Don't be a super parent—learn to ask for help.
* Enjoy yourself—go to a museum or some place fun (the baby won't mind).
* Wear a snuggly around the house so you can get things done and keep the baby warm, happy and quiet.
* And above all, remember: it's a marathon, not a sprint. So always look at the big picture; one less-than-perfect feeding or skipped nap isn't the end of the world.

Gymnastics & Play

If your kid loves to tumble, run and jump, check out these classes. But know what you're looking for first; while your child doesn't need to be a budding Olga Korbut, some of these programs are actually pre-gymnastics programs that are geared towards continued training in the sport. "Developmental gymnastics"—essentially, noncompetitive gymnastics—focuses on basic skills, coordination, balance and strength. Some classes are built around an obstacle course format on real gym equipment for younger kids, with increasingly advanced gymnastics for grade school children and competitive gymnastics for older children. Some other programs are really more play classes and some involve an introduction to the nuts and bolts of sports, such as throwing and catching. But the common theme is that almost all of them involve movement, tumbling and stretching.

BEDFORD HILLS
American Gymnastics
317 Railroad Ave. (914) 241-1997

Preschool classes include "Mom & Me I" *(1½-2½ years)*, "Mom & Me II" *(2½-3½)*, "Ameri-Cubs" *(3-4)* and "Ameri-Bears" *(4-5)*. There is a special program just for 5-year-olds. Programs for older kids *(6-12)* are grouped by age and ability. This facility also offers competitive gymnastics.

BRIARCLIFF MANOR
Club Fit for Kids
584 North State Rd. (914) 762-3444
www.clubfit.com

There are a wide variety of classes for kids, from basic tumbling to introductions to various sports. Classes include "Just for 3s," an introduction to sports and games, "Kindersport" *(age 5)* and "Junior Kinder Sports" *(4)*, which focus on physical and creative movement, and "A Little More Sports" *(5-8)*, which includes kickball, soccer, floor hockey and more.

CHAPPAQUA
World Cup Gymnastics
170 Hunts Ln. (914) 238-4967
www.worldcupgymnastics.com

Gymnastics classes for ages 3 months to 18 years, including "Romperee" parent/child classes (*3-30 months*), preschool classes (*2-5 years*) focusing on early gymnastic skills, and recreational programs (*5-14 years*) to develop beginner through advanced gymnastic skills. There are also Competitive Teams and Exhibition Teams (*6-18*).

CORTLANDT MANOR
Gymnastics City
2121 Crompond Rd. (914) 734-1616

Gymnastics classes for ages 18 months to 12 years. "Mom & Tot" (*18 months-3 years*) and preschool classes (*3-5 years*) are based on an obstacle course format. General classes for girls (*6-9, 10-13 and 14+*) and boys (*6-8 and 9+*) provide instruction on Olympic events.

Gymtime
Pike Plaza, Rte. 6 (914) 241-8650

They offer parent/child recreation programs, including "Hello World," (*3-11 months*), "First Steps" (9-17 months), "Toddlers" (*13-24 months*), "Runners" (18-30 months) and "Jumpers" (*30-48 months*). Classes focus on exercise and movement, and include songs, obstacle courses and parachute play. The unlimited class policy means that if you register for the class of your choice, you can attend any other classes in your child's age group at no additional charge.

CROTON-ON-HUDSON
Straddles Gymnastics
420 S. Riverside Ave. (914) 271-2400

"Split Peas" (*ages 18 months-3 years*), "Tumble Weeds" (*ages 3-5*), and general classes for ages 5-18, separated by age and ability.

HARRISON
International School of Gymnastics (ISG)
151 Crotona Ave. (914) 835-0010

Gymnastics classes for ages 10 months–14 yrs. Classes requiring a caregiver include "Tumbling Bunnies" *(10-18 months)*, "Gyminy Crickets" *(1½-2½ years)* and "Chipmunks" *(2½ -3½)*. For older children there is "Pre-School Girls & Boys" *(ages 3-5)*, as well as age-appropriate classes for ages 5-6, 6-7, 8-12 and 12-14.

HAWTHORNE
Westchester Gymnastics & Dance
5 Skyline Dr. (914) 592-2324

Preschool classes include "Parent & Tot" *(18 months-3 years)*, "Beginner Gym" *(3½-4)*, and "Advance Gym" *(4-5)*. They also offer recreational classes *(ages 4-18)* and a competitive team *(6-17)*.

JEFFERSON VALLEY
Club Fit for Kids
1 Lee Blvd. (914) 245-4040
www.clubfit.com

See the listing under Briarcliff Manor for information.

Gymboree
3631 Hill Blvd. & Rte. 6 (866) 477-3700
www.gymboree.com

Pre-gymnastics, play and movement classes, including "GymBabies" *(0-6 months)*, "GymCrawlers" *(6-12 months)*, "GymWalkers" *(10-18 months)*, "GymRunners" *(14-28 months)*, "GymExplorers" *(2 years)* and "GymKids" *(3-5 years)*. Most classes include time on the play equipment, parachute time, songs and bubble time.

MOHEGAN LAKE
Dynamic Gymnastics
1949 E. Main St. (914) 528-5437

"Terrific Twos" *(18 months-3 years, with caregiver)*, pre-school and kindergarten classes, and recreational gymnastics for ages 5-14, separated by age and ability. This facility also offers advanced classes and team gymnastics.

MOUNT KISCO
Gymtime
195 N. Bedford Rd. *(in the Manufacturer's Outlet Center)*
(914) 241-8650

See the listing under Cortlandt Manor for information.

Jodi's Gym
25 Hubbels Dr. (914) 244-8811

Gymnastics classes for ages 12 months–12 years. "Mommy & Me" *(9 months-walking, 12-17 months, 18-24 months, 25-30 months and 30-35 months)* incorporates running, jumping, climbing, stretching and tumbling. "Tumbling Tots" *(3-4 years and 4-5 years)* focuses on developmental gymnastics, including basic skills. "Kindergym" *(age 5)* focuses on fundamental gymnastics skills. For older children, they offer "Girls Developmental Gymnastics" and "Girls Advanced Gymnastics" *(ages 6-12)*, grouped by age and ability.

61

NEW ROCHELLE
Supreme Dance & Gymnastics
255 Main St. (914) 636-2310
www.supremedance.com

A wide variety of classes for kids of all ages. "Fun Together," *(18 months-3½ years)*, allows parent and child to explore movement, balance and perception through gymnastics and dance activities. Older kids can take classes in gymnastics, tumbling and cheerleading. Supreme also provides private and semiprivate lessons and has a competitive gymnastics team.

PELHAM
Gym Dandy
1415 Pelhamdale Ave. *(Christ Church)* (914) 422-9123

Full-hour classes for ages 6 months-3½ years, including warm-up exercises, songs, puppets, arts and crafts, and parachute play.

Spotlight Gymnastics
901 Pelhamdale Ave. (914) 738-7305
www.spotlightgym.com

"Parents and Tots" (*ages 2-3*) focuses on introductory gymnastics. Class programs (*3-15, grouped by age and ability*) develop basic gymnastics skills. "Pre-Team" (*7+*) prepares students for competition.

POUND RIDGE
Tumble Bugs
55 Westchester Ave. (914) 764-4765

Gymnastics and pre-gymnastics classes for ages 6 months-6 years. For the younger set, there are "Mini Bugs" (*6-12 months*), "Baby Bugs" (*12-18 months*) and "Snuggle Bugs" (*18-24 months*), all requiring caregiver participation. "Tumble Bugs" (*2's, 3-4, 4-5, 5-6; 2-year-olds class require a caregiver*) movement education classes grouped by age and are focused on developing confidence, physical ability and coordination.

SCARSDALE
Gymboree
450 Central Park Ave. (866) 477-3700
www.gymboree.com

See the listing under Jefferson Valley for information.

Gymtime
1 Heathcote Rd. (*Scarsdale Congregational Church*)
(914) 241-8650

See the listing under Cortlandt Manor for information.

The Little Gym
777 White Plains Rd. (914) 722-0072
www.thelittlegym.com

Parent & Infant/Toddler classes include "Birds" *(8-17 months)*, "Beasts" *(18-26 months)* and "Super Beasts" *(27-35 months)*. Preschool, Kindergarten and Grade School classes include "Funny Bugs" *(3-5 years)*, "Giggle Worms" *(4-5 years)* and "Flips" *(6-10 years)*. For older kids, "Cracker Jacks" *(ages 3-5)* incorporates sports skills.

Tumble Bugs
826 Scarsdale Ave. (914) 719-1113

See the listing under Pound Ridge for information.

WHITE PLAINS
Frozen Ropes
55 S. Broadway (914) 993-6355
www.frozenropes.com

In addition to the indoor batting cages and pitcher's mounds, this national chain has classes for kids as young as 2½ years. "Born to Play" *(ages 2½–5)* teaches balance, hand-eye coordination, hitting, throwing and correct terminology. "Basic Fundamentals" *(age 5)* is about advancing skills and techniques.

YONKERS
Gym Cats Gymnastics Center
1 Odell Plaza (914) 965-7676

"Tiny Cats" is divided into three age-appropriate, coed categories that focus on basic movement education: "Mom & Me" *(age 2)*, and classes for ages 3 and 4. "Little Cat" classes *(5-6½)* for boys and girls focus on beginner-level skills. "Big Cat" classes *(6½ and up)* for boys and girls concentrate on skills and routines. There are also "Super Cat" girls' and boys' classes, by invitation only, and Cheerleading and Acrobatics for ages 12 and up.

PUTNAM COUNTY
Gym Magic
Brewster Business Park, Rte. 22, Brewster (845) 278-2076

Preschool classes include "Parent & Tot" (*one for children 18 months-2½ years, and one for 3½-4*), and "Advanced Gym". They also offer recreational classes (*4-18*) and a competitive team (*6-17*).

ROCKLAND COUNTY
New York Sports Club for Kids
3565 Palisades Center Dr. West Nyack (845) 358-1818
www.nysc.com

They offer many recreational athletic programs, including: "Mini Gymi's" (*6-36 months*), a parent/tot class; "Gymtastics" (*1-15 years*), a basic gymnastics skills class; "Cardio Kids" (*3-6*), an age-appropriate sports skills development class; "Dancexperience" (*3-15*); "Cheertastics" (*5-15*); "Kickboxing Kids" (*6-12*) and "Kidspin Theatre" (*8-15*).

CONNECTICUT
Gymboree
31 Mill Plain Rd., Danbury (866) 477-3700
106 Commerce Rd., Stamford (203) 696-1115
www.gymboree.com

See listing under Jefferson Valley for information.

Tumble Bugs
6 Riverside Ave., Riverside (203) 637-3303

See the listing under Pound Ridge for information.

Music

There's no question that children love music and moving around. Perhaps that's why there are so many places that offer music classes here in Westchester. The classes tend to fall within four general styles: Music & Movement, Kindermusik, Dalcroze Eurhythmics and the Suzuki Method. In the first three types of classes, children and parents or caregivers explore rhythm and tonal patterns, musical styles and simple musical instruments. Kids and parents not only listen and sing or play along with the musical selections, but also have a chance to get down and boogie. Some classes use old favorites, some use original music. Some teachers play the guitar, piano or autoharp as children sing along, and some teachers have an accompanist. A number of classes are grouped by age to include developmentally appropriate activities, while others are mixed-age classes (*clearly better for parents wanting to enroll two children of different ages in the same class*). And some classes provide you with a CD and other materials to use at home.

The fourth type of class, those using the Suzuki method, offer a more formal style of teaching in which children use scaled-down instruments like pianos, guitars or violins. This method combines listening, proper technique, repetition, reinforcement and active parent involvement. If you feel you have a budding Beethoven on your hands, this may be the right choice for you.

Some programs believe children will benefit most from a highly structured environment. They may expect children to remain seated at certain times and encourage children and parents or caregivers to follow a specific routine. Other programs believe children will benefit just by being in the room and are less focused on getting twelve toddlers to bang their drums "just so." To find out which style works best for you, check out a few different classes prior to signing up. Almost every program allows a free preview class if you make a reservation in advance.

Remember, these classes are designed for young children. You may find the songs or the teacher painfully corny, but the true test of a great teacher is how the child responds. Also keep in mind that the more into it you are, the more into it your child will be, so just *(rock and)* roll with it, baby. In addition to the listings by town, below, the following two music classes are offered at numerous Westchester locations.

MUSIC TOGETHER
www.musictogether.com

Mixed-age music and movement classes for children ages 0-4, with their parents or caregivers. Classes are forty-five minutes long and the program includes a CD, tape, songbook and parent education guide. This is a franchise with many locations, so call the contact number for your area *(listed below)* to get more information on the classes nearest you:

Northern Westchester *(Croton Falls, Katonah, Mahopac, Peekskill, Yorktown Heights):* (914) 788-1559
Southern Westchester *(Dobbs Ferry, Harrison, Larchmont, Mamaroneck, Pelham, Tarrytown, Tuckahoe, White Plains):* (914) 961-1364
Chappaqua, Cross River, Pound Ridge: (914) 378-5040
Croton-on-Hudson: (914) 690-9180
Mount Pleasant, Valhalla: (914) 747-8545

MUSICAL MUNCHKINS
(914) 771-7000

In this music and movement program classes are divided by age, as follows: "Baby Munchkins" *(6-11 months)*, "Music for 1's" *(12-24 months)*, "Music for 2's" *(24-36 months)*, "Music for 3's and 4's," "Music for 4's" and "Friends & Family" *(14-48 months)*. Classes are forty-five minutes long and usually include familiar songs that you and your children will recognize. There are locations in Armonk, Bronxville, Dobbs Ferry, Larchmont, Mamaroneck, Mt. Kisco, New Rochelle, Pawling, Pleasantville, Rye, Scarsdale and White Plains.

CHAPPAQUA
Amadeus Conservatory
201 King St. (914) 238-0388

These classes are limited to six children and feature the use of real instruments such as violins, recorders, ukuleles, drums and accordions. In addition to the teacher, there is a classroom accompanist. Parent or caregiver participation is obviously essential. While the youngest children may only get a taste of how to play these instruments, as they grow they may develop a real appetite for music.

CORTLANDT MANOR
Musictime
Pike Plaza, Rte. 6 (914) 241-8650

This music and movement program is created for children ages 9 months-4 years. Classes are multi-aged and limited to ten children. This program has a unique unlimited class policy that allows you to go to any other classes at no additional charge. The program cost includes a book, CD and tape.

EASTCHESTER
Crestwood Music
453 White Plains Rd. (914) 961-3497
www.crestwoodmusic.com

This facility focuses primarily on private lessons, but there are some Kindermusik classes available: "Kindermusik Beginnings" *(18 months-3 years)* and "Growing with Kindermusik" *(3-4)*.

JEFFERSON VALLEY
Gymboree Music
3631 Hill Blvd. & Rte. 6 (866) 477-3700
www.gymboree.com

Music & Movement classes broken into various age groups, including "Quarter Notes" *(6–18 months)*, "Half Notes" *(16-30 months)* and "Whole Notes" *(2½-5 years)*.

KATONAH
Amadeus Conservatory
25 Valley Rd. (914) 232-8808

See the listing under Chappaqua for more information.

LARCHMONT
Larchmont Music Academy
2106 Boston Post Rd. (914) 833-8941
www.larchmontmusicacademy.com

The Kindermusik program is available for children from birth to 6 years. The classes are divided by age into "Village" *(0-18 months)*, "Our Time" *(18 months-3 years)*, "Growing" *(3½ -4½)* and "Young Child" *(4½ -6)*. Classes are forty-five minutes long for younger children and an hour for older ones. Home materials are also distributed.

MOUNT KISCO
Jodi's Gym
25 Hubbels Dr. (914) 244-8811

Music & Movement in the truest sense, these music classes are held in a gym. There are a wide variety of classes, separated by age, and all have live music. "Mommy & Me Music & Movement" is for children from 9 months to walking age. "Mommy & Me Gym & Music Combo," an hour-and-fifteen-minute class with a story and snack dividing the music portion from the gym time, is separated into sections for children 12-17 months, 18-24 months, 25-35 months, and 3-4 years. There is also a Manhattan location.

Musictime
195 N. Bedford Rd. *(in the Manufacturer's Outlet Center)* (914) 241-8650

See the listing under Cortlandt Manor for information.

Northern Westchester Center for the Arts
272 N. Bedford Rd. (914) 241-6922
www.nwcaonline.org

A wide variety of music classes, including "Mommy and Me Music" *(18 months-3 years)* and "Music and Make Believe" *(3-5)*.

MOUNT VERNON
Mount Vernon Music Academy
199 N. Columbus Ave. (914) 664-2849
www.hbms.org/mount.htm

A branch of the Hoff-Barthelson Music School *(listed under Scarsdale)*, this program is housed at the First Presbyterian Church. They offer the same types of programs as Hoff-Barthelson, including Dalcroze Eurhythmics, Singing & Movement and Suzuki classes.

NEW ROCHELLE
Joy of Music
1270 North Ave. (914) 654-8753

Programs are available for children 9 months and older. Classes are broken up by age into "Your Baby Needs Music" *(9 months-2 years and 2-3½)*, "Preschool Music Program" *(3½-5½)*, "Fun with Pianos" *(5½-8)* and "Fun with Guitar" *(5½-8)*. They also offer private instruction in flute, guitar and piano as well as classes for special needs children.

OSSINING
Mike Risko Music School
103 Croton Ave. (914) 762-8757
www.mikeriskomusicschool.com

This music school has Kindermusik programs for children from birth to 5 years old. They are divided into "Kindermusik Village" *(newborn-1½ years)*, "Kindermusik Our Time" *(1½-3)* and "Kindermusik Imagine That!" *(3-5)*.

PELHAM
Joy of Music
451 Esplanade Ave. (914) 654-8753

See the listing under New Rochelle for more information.

RYE
Rye Arts Center
51 Milton Rd. (914) 967-0700
www.ryeartscenter.org

"Playing with Music" for 3-year-olds teaches through rhythmic play and musical games. In "Fun with Melody & Rhythm" (*for ages 4-5½*) children are introduced to the basics of music and rhythm using a Suzuki-based method. Children in this class must have group experience and know the alphabet. In "Rise, Sing & Act" (*ages 6 and up*) children sing and act out Broadway, pop and children's songs. Suzuki classes are offered for guitar, violin and piano. This facility also offers some unique music and art combination classes where preschoolers listen and move to music, then participate in an art project based on that musical theme. Private lessons are also available.

SCARSDALE
Belle School of Music
1088 Central Park Ave. (914) 961-5511

This is a more "serious" Kindermusik program for children 2 years and older. Here every child has his or her own mini piano as well as other smaller-sized instruments. Class size ranges from four to eight children. They use an exclusive "magnet system" to teach children to play and read music. Each session has classes that meet once a week for four months. Books and supplies are included.

Gymboree Music
450 Central Park Ave. (866) 477-3700
www.gymboree.com

See the listing under Jefferson Valley for more information.

Hoff-Barthelson Music School
25 School Ln. (914) 723-1169
www.hbms.org

This is a more structured setting where children enjoy singing and movement while learning other skills like following directions and taking turns. The first class they offer is "Guppies" *(12-18 months)* for thirty minutes. Starting with children at age 1, they offer classes in Dalcroze Eurhythmics as follows: "Mother/Child" for 1-2 year olds for forty minutes, "Eurhythmics for 3-4-year-olds" for forty-five minutes and "Musicianship for 4-5-year-olds," also for forty-five minutes. There are recorder classes for young children as well as Suzuki programs for violin, viola, cello and piano for children ages 4 years and older. Lastly, there is a certified preschool center for 3 and 4-year-olds offering two or three-hour classes, depending on the age group.

Joy of Music
One Heathcote Rd. *(Congregational Church)* (914) 654-8753

See the listing under New Rochelle for more information.

Scarsdale Ballet Studio
696 White Plains Rd. (914) 725-8754

This dance facility also offers a "Music 1...2...3!!" program for children ages 18 months to 4½ years and their parents or caregivers. You and your child will sing, dance, play instruments and have a snack and story. Classes are limited to eight students and are divided by age group.

WHITE PLAINS
Belle School of Music
283 Tarrytown Rd. (914) 287-0066

See the listing under Scarsdale for more information.

Music Conservatory of Westchester
216 Central Ave. (914) 761-3900
www.musicconservatory.org

The Music Conservatory of Westchester offers classes, group lessons and individual instruction. For younger kids, classes include "Music & Movement" *(2½ -3½)*, "Pre-School Music" *(3½ -5½)*, and Suzuki classes for violin, piano and cello *(4+)*, and group lessons for violin, piano, recorder and guitar *(5-8)*

YONKERS
Belle School of Music
1537 Central Park Ave.
(914) 961-5511

See the listing under Scarsdale for more information.

CONNECTICUT
Gymboree Music
31 Mill Plain Rd., Danbury (866) 477-3700
106 Commerce Rd., Stamford (203) 696-1115
www.gymboree.com

See the listing under Jefferson Valley for more information.

Savvy Suggestion

Save cardboard rolls from toilet paper and paper towels. You and your child can decorate them with stickers, markers and paint or glued-on objects.

Put some beans or rice inside the roll, and cover the ends with tin foil and seal them with rubber bands to make a maraca.

Or, just let your child use the tube as a "horn" by singing and tooting into it as you march around the house.

Arts & Crafts

Ever since Martha Stewart let us know that there is, indeed, a right and a wrong way to glue rubber stars onto a piece of wood, classes that specialize in arts and crafts projects have multiplied exponentially. Of course, this may also have something to do with the fact that when it comes to paint, clay and glue, "better your place than mine" is usually a parent's sentiment. Either way, here are places where your children can create to their hearts' content. You'll have new *objets d'art* to proudly display around your home, and you won't have to pick sparkles out of the carpet for the next two years.

CHAPPAQUA
New Castle Art Center
939 Hardscrabble Rd. (914) 238-3606
www.newcastle-ny.org/artcenter.html

Classes in art, woodworking and ceramics for ages 2-13.

CORTLANDT
Croton-Cortlandt Center for the Arts
293B Furnace Dock Rd. (914) 739-4320
www.cccarts.org

A variety of classes for ages 3-17 *(some require a caregiver)*, including "Clay Creations," "Young at Art" and "Authors and Illustrators." Workshops include "Marvelous Mobiles" and "Make Your Own Musical Instrument."

DOBBS FERRY
Art In Us
145 Palisade St. (914) 591-5377
www.artinusonline.com

Multimedia classes for ages 2-13 *(some require a caregiver)*.

Hot Mud Studio
145 Palisade St. (914) 478-2762

Pottery classes for ages 7-18 and "Clay Together on Saturday Mornings," a pottery class for ages 5 and up, with a caregiver.

HASTINGS-ON-HUDSON
Messy Art
6 Circle Dr. (914) 478-0756

A variety of classes for ages 13-30 months, including multimedia art, dancing and movement, and singing.

JEFFERSON VALLEY
Gymboree Arts
3631 Hill Blvd. & Rte. 6 (866) 477-3700
www.gymboree.com

Multimedia classes include Gym Arts I *(for ages 18 months-2½ years)* and Gym Arts II *(2½-5)*.

KATONAH
Katonah Art Center & Gallery
77 Bedford Rd. (914) 232-4843
www.katonahartcenter.com

This center has classes for ages 2-18 *(some require a caregiver to attend)*. "Little Rembrandts" *(2-3)* includes many materials and techniques. In "Petite Picassos" *(4-6)* children create a masterpiece each week. Classes for older children include mixed media, drawing and painting, and cartooning.

LARCHMONT
Children's Creative Corner
7 Addison St. (914) 833-2880

A variety of classes for ages 5-14, including painting, drawing and ceramics.

Your Art Out
2005 Palmer Ave. (914) 833-2321
www.paintyourartout.com

The classes offered for ages 5-13 include drawing, painting, cartooning, stained glass and mosaics.

MOUNT KISCO
Northern Westchester Center of the Arts
272 N. Bedford Rd. (914) 241-6922
www.nwcaonline.org

A variety of classes for ages 2-14, including "Mommy & Me Art," (2-3), "Discovery Art Workshop" (3-5) and "Journey Through Art" (3-5)

PELHAM
Pelham Art Center
155 Fifth Ave. (914) 738-2525

A variety of classes for ages 4-18 have included Mommy & Me, crafts, ceramics, drama and dance. There are also workshops for children in various media, coordinated with gallery openings.

PORT CHESTER
Clay Art Center of Westchester
40 Beech St. (914) 937-2047

Ceramics classes for ages 7-12.

RYE
Rye Arts Center
51 Milton Rd. (914) 967-0700
www.ryeartscenter.org

The classes for kids ages 3-18 include "Art for Three & Four," "Pre-K Clay" and "Creative Mixed Media," but they vary by season so contact them to find out what classes are currently being offered.

SCARSDALE
Gymboree Arts
450 Central Park Ave. (866) 477-3700
www.gymboree.com

See the listing under Jefferson Valley for more information.

Young At Art
1088 Central Park Ave. (914) 723-9229

Multimedia classes including "Mommy & Me" (*ages 2½-3, 3-4, and 4-5*).

WHITE PLAINS
Westchester Art Workshop
196 Central Park Ave. (914) 684-0094

A variety of classes for ages 6-13, including clay, jewelry making and painting.

CONNECTICUT
Greenwich Art Society
299 Greenwich Ave., Greenwich (203) 629-1533

Multimedia classes for ages 7-10.

Gymboree Arts
31 Mill Plain Rd., Danbury (866) 477-3700
www.gymboree.com

See the listing under Jefferson Valley for more information.

ROCKLAND COUNTY
Rockland Center For The Arts
27 S. Greenbush Rd., West Nyack (845) 358-0877
www.rocklandartcenter.org

A variety of classes for ages 3-18, including mixed media, ceramics, painting and drawing. There are also parent/child workshops where you can learn to make things like mosaics, snow globes and wrapping paper.

PUTNAM COUNTY
Garrison Arts Center
23 Garrison's Landing, Garrison (845) 424-3960
www.garrisonartcenter.org

A variety of classes for ages 5-12, including pottery, painting, drawing, mixed media and sculpture. They also offer workshops and school vacation camps.

Savvy Savings

Instead of going to the "brand name stores," hit the discounters like dollar stores, Odd Jobs Lot and the large warehouse clubs for huge savings on things like toys, arts & crafts materials and wrapping paper.

Dance

Few of us can resist the opportunity to see our daughters in frilly pink tutus at least once. And for those of us with sons, this is the perfect way to impart some semblance of rhythm and coordination to them so that they can be the coolest ones on the dance floor when they get older. With irresistible cuteness and coolness on offer, it is not surprising that there are tons of dance classes in Westchester. The style of dance varies—some facilities focus exclusively on ballet, while others offer a wide range of classes, including less traditional forms like hip-hop, Broadway, Irish step and acrobatic.

BEDFORD HILLS
Westchester Theater Dance Academy
54 Babbitt Rd. (914) 241-4410
www.peti-paw.com

This dance company has a program designed specifically for preschoolers that includes classes like "Baby Dance" *(for ages 2½-3)* and a "Pas de Preschool" with tap, jazz and ballet arts. These unique classes teach not only movement but also the cultural, historical and artistic backgrounds of dance. Children give their artistic interpretation through an art project based on the theme of the music. Beyond recreational classes, the school also offers programs for theater dance, ballet, jazz, hip-hop and tap. Every spring the students perform at the Yorktown Stage.

CHAPPAQUA
Ballet des Enfants
18 S. Greeley Ave. (914) 428-3230

"Fairytale Ballet" is a traditional ballet-based creative movement program with a unique twist. The first half of the class is spent on terms and movements followed by a story. The second half of the class is spent in costume, "dancing out" that story using props. For little ones, this program offers a Mommy & Me class *(age 2)* and an independent class *(2½-3½)* called "First Steps," followed by

"Leaps & Bounds" *(3-4)*. "Classical Kids" *(5-6)* is a pre-ballet program. There are also ballet classes for 7-year-olds.

Dance Emotions
75 S. Greeley Ave. (914) 238-8974
www.danceemotions.com

This facility is in its twenty-first year of operation. Their style is child-friendly but structured, and even the youngest student will learn some "real" dance moves. There's "Pre-Dance" *(2½-5)*, "Ballet/Tap" *(4-5)*, "Kinderkids" *(5-6)* and "Ballet/Theatrical Jazz/Tap Combo" *(7 and up)*. From there, children can take hour-long classes or "intensives" in ballet, tap, theatrical jazz and hip-hop, and there's pointe for advanced dancers. There is a year-end show at the Horace Greeley School Theater.

Steffi Nossen School of Dance
Orchard Ridge Rd. *(First Congregational Church)*
(914) 328-1900
www.steffinossen.org

This school offers a wide range of classes for all ages and levels. 2-year-olds *(with a parent or caregiver)* can enjoy a creative movement "Mommy & Me" or "Classical Story Ballet," class where they'll learn classical ballet movement and vocabulary by dancing to stories using props and costumes. These classes are also offered independently for 3-, 4-, and 5-year-olds. This dance school has preschool classes in creative movement, modern, tap and, for slightly older children, hip-hop, theater movement, Broadway, jazz and, of course, ballet.

CORTLANDT MANOR
Dance Magic
2050 E. Main St. (914) 736-1110

A smaller, "boutique" studio that believes in the magic of dance. "Move & Groove" *(age 3)* features tumbling, obstacle courses, instruments and props, ballet, jazz and creative movement. "Ballerinas to Be" *(4)* is a combination of tumbling, jazz, ballet, and instruments and props. "Tumble Jazz" *(5-6)* focuses on building skill and coordination while teaching the basics of dance. Classes are limited to eight kids. Students have the opportunity to join the "Dance Team," which performs at the Westchester County Center every other year and also travels to and performs at places like Disney World.

EASTCHESTER
Studio B. Dance Center
375 White Plains Rd. (914) 793-2799

This facility offers pre-ballet/creative movement *(ages 2-3)*, ballet/tap *(4-5)*, and ballet, tap and jazz classes *(6+)*. There are also modern dance classes with instrumental and percussive music *(5+)* and hip-hop *(8+)*. The "Pre-Company" program *(6+)* is for those children who are serious about studying dance *(classes are two hours long)* and wish to participate in live performances.

HASTINGS-ON-HUDSON
Broadway Training Center
10 Washington Ave. (914) 478-5825
www.broadwaytraining.com

Preschool programs *(ages 3-4 and 4-5)* include pre-ballet, boys-only ballet and pre-performance *(for budding actors and actress)*. For older children *(ages 5 and up)*, there are classes in ballet, jazz, tap, hip-hop, acting, singing and musical theater. Junior Ensemble *(6-12)* and Senior Ensemble *(12-18)* meet at least three days a week and build up to live performances of Broadway shows at a local theater.

On Hudson Fitness & Dance Studio
558 Warburton Ave. (914) 478-0508

A variety of classes, including "Mom & Tot" *(6 months-2 years)*, "Creative Ballet" *(3-4)*, "Creative Jazz" *(3½-5)*, pre-ballet and pre-ballet/tap *(4-5)*.

LARCHMONT
A Dance Studio
2094 Boston Post Rd. (914) 834-2432

This studio offers "Preschool Beginner Classes" *(ages 3-5)*, a combination of creative movement and some tap, and "Tu-Tu Ballet" *(3-4)*. As children get older and more confident *(5-9)*, they can opt for ballet or a tap/jazz combo class. There are also hip-hop classes for ages 8 and up.

Lorna London School of Ballet
1810 Palmer Ave. (914) 834-4005

It's "Pure Ballet" at this venerable school. Most classes are still taught by Lorna herself, who has over fifty years of experience, making her a classy classic. There are pre-ballet *(ages 3-4)* and ballet *(5-10)* classes, and each class is divided by age and ability.

MAMARONECK
Ballet des Enfants
546 E. Boston Post Rd. *(United Methodist Church)*
(914) 428-3230

See the listing under Chappaqua for more information.

81

Dance Cavise
273 Halstead Ave. (914) 381-5222
www.dancecavise.com

This facility offers "Creative Movement" *(ages 2-4)*; pre-ballet, tap or jazz *(5)*; and ballet, tap, or jazz *(6+)*. As kids get older they can also take other types of lessons like hip-hop, modern and pointe *(for advanced dancers)*.

Steffi Nossen School of Dance
168 Boston Post Rd. *(St. Thomas Church)* (914) 328-1900
www.steffinossen.org

See the listing under Chappaqua for more information.

MOUNT KISCO
Northern Westchester Center for the Arts
272 N. Bedford Rd. (914) 241-6922
www.nwcaonline.org

There are a wide variety of classes, including Mommy & Me *(2-3 years)*; "Dance Dramatics" *(3-4)*; "Creative Movement" *(3 -5)*, a combination of ballet, modern and jazz; "Pre-Ballet" *(4-5)*; "Dance Forms 1 & 2" *(4-5 and 5-6)*, an introduction to ballet, modern and jazz; and "I Got Rhythm" *(ages 4-5)*, a music appreciation and dance class. They also offer ballet, jazz, tap, boy's tap, hip-hop and Irish step classes *(6+)*.

The Dance Connection of Mt. Kisco
35 Main St. (914) 244-4224

This facility offers "Creative Movement" *(ages 3-4)*, "Kindergarten Ballet, Jazz & Tap" *(5-6)*, "First/Second Grade Ballet" *(7-8)* and "Jazz & Broadway Tap" *(7-8)*.

MOUNT VERNON
Steffi Nossen School of Dance
Lincoln Ave. *(United Methodist Church)* (914) 328-1900
www.steffinossen.org

See the listing under Chappaqua for more information.

NEW ROCHELLE
Rooftop Rhythms Dance Studio
10 S. Division St., #7 (914) 576-6027
www.rooftoprhythms.com

A newer studio that has classes ranging from those you can do with your 18-month-old to those you may want to take yourself. For the littlest ones, there is "Mommy & Me" *(18 months-2 years)* and "2-Too Cute," a year-long class for *(as the name suggests)* 2-year-olds that teaches a combination of ballet and tap and culminates with an end-of-the-year recital. For older kids, there is tap/ballet *(3-4, 5-6 and 7-9)*, jazz, tap, and ballet *(7-9)*, hip-hop *(7-9)* and boys-only hip-hop *(7-9)*.

OSSINING
Logrea Dance Academy
2 Dale Ave. (914) 941-2939
www.logreadance.com

This academy teaches a wide variety of ballet classes, including "Pre-Ballet" *(ages 3-4, only children out of diapers)*, "Elementary 1" *(4-5)*, "Elementary 2" *(5-6)*, "Ballet 1" *(6-8)* and "Ballet 2" *(7-9)*. For kids 7 and up, they teach other dance styles, including tap, jazz and modern.

PELHAM
Ballet Arts/The Performing Arts Center of Southern Westchester
504 Fifth Ave. (914) 738-8300
www.ballet-arts.net

This program has classes for a wide variety of ages and styles. Programs include: Ballet *(ages 3-4, 4 and 5-6)*, Ballet 1A *(7-11)*, Ballet 1 *(7-9, with prior experience)*, Tap/Jazz *(6-9)*, Tap/Jazz Level 1 *(8-11)*, Irish Step *(4, 5-6, 6+)* and Modern Dance *(7-11)*. There is also a Musical Theater class, which includes singing, acting and dancing *(7-11)*.

83

Ballet Atlantic Academy *(formerly Mid-Atlantic Ballet School & Co.)*
629 Fifth Ave. (914) 738-7210

If you want authentic, disciplined ballet training for your child this school may be the one for you. The youngest students can participate in the "Kindergarten of Dance" program *(ages 4-5)*, which gets children ready to learn ballet and familiarizes them with dance terms and basic movements. "Basic Ballet" *(6-7½)* involves both barre and center work in a one-hour class. The more advanced ballet classes *(7½+)* can meet two to three times a week. The Academy puts on several performances a year, including an annual presentation of "The Nutcracker."

The Beverly Dance Studio
139 Wolfs Ln. (914) 738-5277

This studio offers classes for ages 2 through adult. If your child is okay with separating from you, he can take a "Pre-Ballet/Tap for 2's" class, which includes a performance at the end. They also offer ballet, tap, jazz and hip-hop classes that are divided by age.

PLEASANTVILLE
Steffi Nossen School of Dance
The Richard G. Rosenthal YM-YWHA, 600 Bear Ridge Rd.
(914) 328-1900
www.steffinossen.org

See the listing under Chappaqua for more information.

PORT CHESTER
Westchester Performing Arts Center
181 Westchester Ave. (914) 690-1501

The Center offers a variety of classes for young children, including a Mommy & Me program *(ages 18 months-2 years)*, "Creative Movement" *(2½-3)*, "Ballet/Tap Combo" *(3-4 and 5-6)* and "Ballet/Jazz Combo" *(3-4 and 5-6)*. For older kids, there is ballet *(5, 6 and 7)*, jazz *(6-7)*, acrobatics and tumbling *(6-7)*, boys' jazz *(6-8)*, lyrical *(9)* and hip-hop *(11-13)*. This center also has advanced programs for children of increasing age and experience.

RYE
Rye Arts Center
51 Milton Rd. (914) 967-0700
www.ryeartscenter.org

In the "Dance Me A Story" class *(age 3)*, children use creative movement to discover how favorite stories can be intertwined with dance. Simple dance techniques are introduced to develop imagination, self-expression and listening skills. Old and new preschool literature is used.

SCARSDALE
Ballet des Enfants
270 Ardsley Rd. *(Greenville Community Church)*
(914) 428-3230

See the listing under Chappaqua for more information.

Central Park Dance
450 Central Park Ave. (914) 723-2940
www.centralparkdance.com

Over a hundred classes in more than ten different styles of dance *(plus acting, aerobics, fitness and voice classes)*. There is a preschool program, starting with "Tot & I" *(ages 2½-3)*, and then classes for ages 3-4, 4-5 and 5-6. Children ages 6 and up can choose from classes in ballet, jazz, hip-hop, funk, theater jazz, modern, tap, ballroom and even belly dancing.

Scarsdale Ballet Studio
696 White Plains Rd. (914) 725-8754

"Creative Ballet" *(ages 3, 4, and 5)* is a creative movement class that focuses on rhythm and coordination as children are introduced to the joy of dance. For older kids, "Pre-Ballet" (6) and "Elementary Level I" (7) focus on classical ballet training and technique. Levels progress from there based on age and ability.

Steffi Nossen School of Dance
Popham Rd. *(Scarsdale Community Baptist Church)*
(914) 328-1900
www.steffinossen.org

See the listing under Chappaqua for more information.

85

SLEEPY HOLLOW
Sleepy Hollow Performing Arts Center
38 Beekman Ave. (914) 333-0663

A variety of styles for a variety of ages, including "Creative Movement" *(ages 3-5)*, ballet *(4-7)*, hip-hop *(6-9)*, pre-ballet/ tap *(4-5)*, boys-only beginning breakdance/hip-hop *(7-12)*, hip-hop/jazz *(5-7, 6-8 and 7-9)* and beginning breakdancing *(6-10)*.

SOUTH SALEM
Dance Cavise "North"
206 Oakridge Commons (914) 533-6501
www.dancecavise.com

See the listing under Mamaroneck for more information.

TARRYTOWN
Tappan Zee Dance Group
27 S. Washington Ave. (914) 631-6692

For the little ones, there is "Creative Movement" *(ages 3-4)*. For older kids, there's "Dance Prep," a pre-ballet class *(5-6)*.

THORNWOOD
Academy of Dance Arts
842 Franklin Ave. (914) 741-5678

They offer classes in ballet, jazz, tap, hip-hop, acrobatic, lyrical *(ballet/modern)* and creative movement. There's also pre-ballet for preschoolers.

WHITE PLAINS
City Center Dance
236 E. Post Rd. (914) 328-1881
www.citycenterdance.com

This facility has creative movement classes *(ages 3-4)*, tap *(5+)*, ballet, jazz and hip-hop *(6+)*.

Steffi Nossen School of Dance

3 Carhart Ave. *(St. Matthews Church)*
216 Central Park Ave. *(Westchester Conservatory of Music)*
(914) 328-1900
www.steffinossen.org

See the listing under Chappaqua for more information.

PUTNAM COUNTY
The Dance Shop
1000 Miller Rd., Mahopac (845) 628-2312

A variety of classes, including "Mommy & Me" *(ages 18 months-2½ years)*, "Creative Movement" *(2½-4)* and combo classes *(4-5)*, such as ballet/creative movement, ballet/tap or ballet/jazz. For older kids *(6+)*, there are classes in ballet, tap, jazz, hip-hop and modern.

PlayZone
1511 Rte. 22, Suite C-21 *(Lake View Shopping Plaza)*, Brewster (845) 279-5378

This indoor play space also offers a wide range of dance classes. For 3- to 4-year-olds there is "Creative Movement," "All That Jazz," "Tiny Taps" and a "Hip-hop" class. For 5- and 6-year-olds there are ballet, jazz, tap and hip-hop, with more advanced versions of those programs for 7- to 11-year-olds. For your little show-stopper they also offer "Broadway Starz" *(for ages 4-6)*.

Martial Arts

One of the great things about studying martial arts is that it teaches children to use their heads before using their hands. As they learn the physical technique of a martial art, they also learn how to cultivate mental attributes such as focus, attention, respect and discipline. You can enroll your child in most programs when she is as young as three and a half, sometimes even younger. And who knows? You may even find yourself donning a "gi" as well.

ARDSLEY
Chai Karate Do
4 American Legion Dr. (914) 674-4893

"Little Dragons" *(ages 5 and under)* is a basic introduction to karate. Classes are then divided by age and skill.

BEDFORD HILLS
Black Dragon's Martial Arts and Fitness Center
717A Bedford Rd. (914) 244-8888
www.blackdragon2K.com

For the little ones, this center offers "Little Dragons" *(ages 3½ and up)*.

HARRISON
Bruce Chung's Tae Kwon Do
250 Halstead Ave. (914) 835-0665
www.brucechung.com

Classes for kids ages 1-8 include "Gym-mini Kick-it Mommy & Me" *(12-24 months and 2-3 years)* and Tae Kwon Do *(3½-5 and 6-8)*.

HASTINGS-ON-HUDSON
N.Y. GOJU Karate Assoc.
558 Warburton Ave. (914) 478-0508

The association offers "Tiny Tigers" Goju Karate *(ages 3-4 and 4-5)*, as well as karate *(5+)*.

LARCHMONT
Larchmont Martial Arts Center
6 Depot Way West (914) 834-1971

The classes for kids at this academy include "Ninjas" *(4-5)*, "Dragons" *(6-7)* and "Eagles" *(8-11)*.

OSSINING
Black Belt Tae Kwon Do
246 S. Highland Ave. *(Arcadian Shopping Center)*
(914) 923-9600

This facility offers "Tiny Little Dragons" *(ages 3-4)*, "Little Dragons" *(4-6)* and a Children's Class *(6-12)*, as well as classes for teens and adults. Students are certified as they move through the ranks. This is a traditional school, but the emphasis is on a fun environment in which to learn proper technique and mindset while building coordination and focus.

MOUNT KISCO
Black Belt Tae Kwon Do
477 Lexington Ave. (914) 241-9400

See the listing under Ossining for more information.

89

PLEASANTVILLE
Asian Tiger Martial Arts
56 Washington Ave. (914) 747-KICK
www.asian-tiger.com

This facility offers "Lil' Tigers" *(ages 3- 4)* for the younger set. For older kids, it offers a multi-discipline blend of martial arts programs *(5+)*.

Black Belt Tae Kwon Do
25 Broadway (914) 769-5600

See the listing under Ossining for more information.

SCARSDALE
Central Park Dance
450 Central Park Ave. (914) 723-2940
www.centralparkdance.com

In addition to a range of dance classes, this facility offers age-specific karate classes *(ages 4-6, 7-9 and 8-12)*.

THORNWOOD
Bushido School of Karate
1008 Broadway (914) 741-1177
www.bushidokarate.com

For younger students, this school offers "Little Eagles" *(ages 28 -40 months)*. For older children, there are karate classes *(4-6 and 7-9)* broken down by age, weight and experience.

WHITE PLAINS
Grand Master Byung Min Kim Taekwondo
60 S. Broadway (914) 428-0085
www.grandmasterbmkim.com

The Grand Master offers Tae Kwon Do for both young children *(ages 3-5)* and older ones *(6-12)*.

YONKERS
Tiger Schulmann's Karate
2500-10 Central Park Ave. *(in the Best Buy Shopping Center)*
(914) 779-4900
www.tsk.com

The "Tiger Cubs" preschool program stresses "advancement and growth based on each child's individual pace." Classes are taught by child care professionals trained to provide motivational instruction. Intermediate and advanced classes are also available as your child's skill increases.

CONNECTICUT
Tiger Schulmann's Karate
2333 Summer St., Stamford *(Ridgeway Shopping Center)*
(203) 969-0352
www.tsk.com

See the listing under Yonkers for information.

PUTNAM COUNTY
Bushido School of Karate
1511 Rt. 22, Brewster (845) 279-8500 *(Lakeview Shopping Center)*
www.bushidokarate.com

See listing under Thornwood for information.

PlayZone
1511 Rte. 22, Suite C-21 *(Lake View Shopping Plaza)*, Brewster
(845) 279-5378

"Creative Karate" *(ages 4-6)* focuses on developing tumbling skills, balance and coordination, as well as covering the basics of karate. "Kung Fu" *(4-6)* involves strength training, aerobics, stretching and self-defense. For older kids *(7-11)*, there are karate and kung fu classes.

Swimming

Swimming classes for babies? Think of them more as aquatic appreciation classes. These programs teach kids to enjoy being in and around water so that they will be more comfortable when they get old enough to really learn strokes, breathing techniques, diving and more. Parents and kids spend about thirty minutes in the pool singing songs, playing games and splashing around. Our husbands both took Saturday morning classes with the boys, which was a great father-son activity for them and gave us a few extra hours of sleep. Although classes are offered at many community centers and health clubs year-round, just make sure you want to be braving the winter temperatures with a damp head and a squirming child. And be forewarned: in most cases even heated pools can often feel pretty chilly, although the children seem to mind a lot less than the parents. During the summer you can also find swimming classes at many of the state, county and municipal swimming facilities, which we listed in the "Pools & Beaches" section of Chapter 6.

BRIARCLIFF MANOR
Club Fit for Kids
584 N. State Rd. (914) 762-3444
www.clubfit.com

Classes for kids ages 6 months and older. "Parent/Infant" (*6-18 months*) and "Parent/Tot" (*19-36 months*) classes focus on interactive water play, fun and songs. For ages 3 and up, classes focus on basic techniques and water safety skills.

JEFFERSON VALLEY
Club Fit for Kids
1 Lee Blvd. (914) 245-4040
www.clubfit.com

See the listing under Briarcliff Manor for information.

MOUNT KISCO
Saw Mill Club
77 Kensico Dr. (914) 241-0797
www.sawmillclub.com

Classes for children from 6 months to 10 years that are age- and level-appropriate. The focus is on improving stroke techniques, acquiring safety skills and increasing water comfort while gaining strength and endurance.

PURCHASE
Purchase College SUNY
Department of Physical Education
735 Anderson Hill Rd. (914) 251-6546

Classes for kids ages 8 months-12 years. Infant and pre-school lessons are taken with a parent or caregiver. The classes for older children focus on primary skills and stroke readiness, development and refinement.

TARRYTOWN
Marymount College of Fordham University
100 Marymount Ave. (914) 332-7445

This "Learn to Swim Program" includes classes for kids ages 2-10, focusing on primary swim skills, strokes, etc. There are also Sunday morning "Family Swims" year-round.

WHITE PLAINS
New York Sports Club for Kids
One N. Broadway (914) 946-0404
www.nysc.com

Classes for kids ages 6 months to 10 years. These learn-to-swim programs integrate learning important safety skills with fun activities.

Foreign Language

It may seem like your child can already say "no" in every conceivable language. But if you want to expand her repertoire, there are many language classes available. Westchester is a popular area for foreign professionals to temporarily relocate to or settle in on a more permanent basis. If that describes your situation, and particularly if you are planning on returning to your original country within a few years, these classes can help your child learn your native language while still attending day school with the neighborhood kids.

CHAPPAQUA
The Language Exchange
83 N. Greeley Ave. (914) 238-2614
www.foreignlanguageexchange.com

They offer classes in nineteen languages for ages 1 year and up. Classes are organized by age and level, depending on the child, and focus on learning through age-appropriate activities.

EASTCHESTER
Language Link
139 Lincoln Ave. (914) 725-1026
www.languagelinkcenter.com

Classes in over ten languages for children ages 10 months and older, organized by age and ability. Also offers Mommy & Me classes in French, Italian and Spanish.

LARCHMONT
Armelle's Language Studio
2 East Ave. (914) 833-0781

Children 6 months and older learn French through songs, allowing them to assimilate the language while having fun. The classes focus on imitation, comprehension and repetition, and include interactive songs, sing-along games, finger-play and puppets.

Peekaboo Learning Center
4 Chatsworth Ave. Suite 4 (914) 833-9754
www.peekaboolearningcenter.com

Classes in French and Spanish for preschool, school-age
children and adults. Children's classes focus on initiation in
the rhythms and sounds of a foreign language, and include
learning basic vocabulary and songs, coloring and games.

RYE
The Little Language League
65 Orchard Ave. (914) 921-9075
www.languageleague.com

The Little Language League stresses learning in context and
adheres to the fundamentals of Montessori philosophy.
"Language Together" is a French or Spanish immersion class
for children ages 6 months-3 years (*with parent or caregiver*). "Language for Kids," for children ages 3-10, develops
French or Spanish language skills through art, music and
theater. "Theater through a Child's Eyes," for ages 3 and up,
introduces children to the performing arts through speech,
movement and song, and is available in English, French and
Spanish.

95

SCARSDALE
Language Workshop
White Plains & Heathcote Rds. (800) 609-5484
www.thibauttechnique.com

"French for Tots" is a structured playgroup for children ages
6 months-3 years (*with parent or caregiver*) that includes
games, songs and more. There are also "French for Tots"
classes that include arts and crafts or music and movement.
"French for Children" (*3-8*) teaches through age-appropriate
games, vocabulary songs and other playful and educational
activities.

WHITE PLAINS
Berlitz Language Center
1 N. Broadway (914) 946-8389
www.languagecenter.berlitz.com/whiteplains

Classes in Spanish and French for children ages 4-11. Kids learn through play, songs, stories and other activities, and learn the new language the same way they learned their first—naturally, through conversation.

CONNECTICUT
The Language Exchange
203 E. Putnam Ave., #10, Cos Cob (203) 422-2024
www.foreignlanguageexchange.com

See the listing under Chappaqua for more information.

Language Workshop
Putnam Ave. & Mason St., Greenwich (800) 609-5484
www.thibauttechnique.com

See the listing under Scarsdale for more information.

,

Culture Club

Museums
Theaters, Concerts & Children's Performances

There comes a time in your child's life when you have to accept that those classical music tapes you've been playing since pre-birth will only get her so far. Now it's time to begin the next phase of your child's cultural education. In Westchester and nearby areas, there are great cultural institutions to share with your kids—so plan a trip to one of these fantastic children's museums or theaters. The listings here are specifically for children or feature children's programs. Obviously New York City is the center of the world when it comes to culture—and being just a short train ride away from the center of the world isn't too shabby.

Museums

Westchester has tons of great resources, but museums for kids isn't one of them—there are only a couple of places in the county that have dedicated children's programs. As of this writing, there is a movement underway to establish a Westchester Children's Museum; if you'd like more information on this effort, visit **www.discoverwcm.org**.

For now, cast the net a bit wider and you'll find numerous places where kids can explore art, science, natural history and much, much more. There are a number of children's museums in surrounding counties that have great activities for kids—some places can keep them busy all day! Also, several of the "grown-up" museums in the area have special children's areas or programs for children. These places are worth the trek.

KATONAH
Katonah Museum of Art
Rte. 22 at Jay St. (914) 232-9555
www.katonah-museum.org

The museum has six major exhibitions each year, as well as
a sculpture garden. The Learning Center, an interactive art
exploration area, hosts a variety of exhibitions, programs
and drop-in activities, including "Tuesdays for Tots." In
addition, there are several three-session parent/child
courses, such as "Create a Memory Box" and "See-and-Do
Art Activities."
Hours: Tuesday –Saturday 10 am–5 pm, Sunday 12–5 pm
Admission: $3 adults, free for members and children under 12

YONKERS
Hudson River Museum/Andrus Planetarium
511 Warburton Ave. (914) 963-4550
www.hrm.org

Westchester's oldest and largest museum features events
for kids. Recent special attractions have included "Funny
Fish," with live creatures from the Hudson River, and "At the
Turning of Time," a mask and puppet show dramatizing the
history of the Hudson River. The Andrus Planetarium has a
variety of shows featuring the constellations, planets and sky.
Hours: May–September, Wednesday–Sunday 12–5 pm
Admission: Museum—$5 adults, $3 children, free for
members; Planetarium—$5 adults *($4 on weekend afternoons)*, $3 children 12 and under
What to Know Before You Go: Friday Star Nites *(7 pm
show)* is free.

MANHATTAN
American Museum of Natural History
(81st & 77th St. Entrances of CPW) (212) 769-5100
www.amnh.org

Kids interested in dinosaurs, birds or fish will love exploring
this museum. The Hall of Ocean Life has just undergone a
major renovation so be sure to check out the ninety-four-

foot-long female blue whale model. The Discovery Room offers a hands-on look at the museum through puzzles and games, artifacts and specimens, scientific challenges and investigations. The museum also offers a variety of programs for kids, and the Space Show at the Rose Center/Hayden Planetarium is fun for all ages.

Hours: Daily 10 am–5:45 pm; the Rose Center is open on Fridays until 8:45 pm; closed Thanksgiving and Christmas Day

Admission: $12 adults, $7 children, free for members; additional fees apply for the Rose Center, Space Show and IMAX theater

What to Know Before You Go: The new Museum Food Court *(lower level)* has sandwiches, pizza, a grill, a salad bar and more. Strollers are not allowed in the Space Theater, but you can leave them outside. Children under 2 are admitted to the Theater free and must sit on their parents' laps.

Children's Museum of the Arts
182 Lafayette St. (212) 941-9198
www.cmany.org

This is a hands-on art museum for children ages 1-12, with activities that include painting, sculpting, building and imagining in many different media. Special exhibits and activities include the "Monet Ball Pond," "Preschool Creative Play Area," "Lines and Shapes," where kids use computer sketch pads to create shapes on a giant color-form wall, and the "Wonder Theater," where children are given a theme and encouraged to design a set, costume and props, which they then use to produce and perform vignettes. The museum has many programs, both registered and walk-in, for young children.

Hours: Daily 10 am–5:45 pm; the Rose Center is open on Fridays until 8:45 pm; closed Thanksgiving and Christmas Day

Admission: $6 per person, free on Thursday 4–6 pm

What to Know Before You Go: The new Museum Food Court *(lower level)* has sandwiches, pizza, a grill, a salad bar and more. Strollers are not allowed in the Space Theater, but you can leave them outside. Children under 2 are admitted to the Theater free and must sit on their parents' laps.

Children's Museum of Manhattan
The Tisch Building, 212 W. 83rd St. (212) 721-1234
www.cmom.org

This museum offers five floors of exhibits such as "Peter Rabbit's Garden: A Beatrix Potter Exhibition," "Where the Wild Things Are: Maurice Sendak In His Own Words" and "Pictures and City Splash." If you have a newborn or toddler, don't miss the "Word Play" exhibit and the "Early Childhood Center." The museum also offers parent/child classes for kids 6 months–3 years, as well as after-school classes for kids 4–12.
Admission: $6 per person, free for children under 1 and members
Hours: Wednesday–Sunday 10 am–5 pm; closed Mondays & Tuesdays except for Martin Luther King Day, Presidents' Day, Memorial Day, Labor Day and Columbus Day
What to Know Before You Go: Strollers must be left at the coat check. No food or beverages are permitted in the Museum.

CONNECTICUT
Bruce Museum of Arts & Sciences
1 Museum Dr., Greenwich (203) 869-0376
www.brucemuseum.org

The art collection may not excite your child, but she may be interested in the museum's natural history exhibits, which include reptiles, fish, butterflies, fossils, and bird and mammal displays. The museum also offers children's programs, including "Look and See: For Young Museum Visitors," a class for kids 3–5 *(with parents or caregivers)* that explores the museum through hands-on experiences, crafts and stories.
Hours: Tuesday–Saturday 10 am–5 pm, Sunday 1–5 pm
Admission: $5 adults, free for children under 5 and members
What to Know Before You Go: There is a great park outside the museum with a playground for toddlers and one for older kids, as well as picnic tables. The Museum is only a five-minute drive from downtown Greenwich, a town filled with great restaurants, stores and two movie theaters. You can really make this trip an all-day event.

Stepping Stones Museum for Children
303 West Ave., Norwalk (203) 899-0606
www.steppingstonesmuseum.org

Exhibits at this museum encourage hands-on exploration
and discovery for children 10 and under, incorporating the
themes of Science and Technology, The Arts, and Culture
and Heritage. Exhibits include "Toddler Terrain" *(for ages 3
and under)*, "Waterscape" *(an interactive water exhibit)*,
"Express Yourself" *(an art center)*, "In the Works" *(a motion
center)* and an exhibit on Connecticut.
Hours: Tuesday–Sunday 10 am–5 pm, Open Mondays
(Memorial Day through Labor Day only) 10 am–5 pm
Admission: $7 per person, free for children under 1
What to Know Before You Go: The museum has a brand
new café featuring child- and adult-friendly breakfast *(cereals,
omelets, etc.)*, lunch *(wraps, salads, pizzas, hot dogs, etc.)*,
and snack offerings *(yogurts, puddings, healthy snacks)* for
visitors. You can also bring your own food and enjoy it at
the indoor eating area or the larger outdoor picnic area.
Smocks are provided at the Waterscape area, but energetic
kids can still get drenched; you may want to bring an extra
set of clothes.

101

NEW JERSEY
Liberty Science Center
Liberty State Park, Jersey City (201) 200-1000
www.lsc.org

This site offers hundreds of interactive exhibits, such as
touch tanks with fish, crabs and environments similar to
those found near the lower Hudson River, and a "Bug Zoo"
crawling with all sorts of creatures. Many activities are
geared towards elementary/middle school kids, but kids 3
and up will have fun here. There are Discovery Rooms on
each floor that are designed for younger explorers, and
scientific demonstrations are presented throughout the
day. There is also a 3D Laser Show and an IMAX theater
(additional fees apply).
Hours: Daily 9:30 am–5:30 pm; closed Thanksgiving and
Christmas Day
Admission: $10 adults, $8 children 2–18, free for children
under 2 and members; $5 parking

What to Know Before You Go: The center is very stroller friendly and has wide aisles for young ones to run around in. Food is available in the Laser Lights Café.

New Jersey Children's Museum
599 Valley Health Plaza, Paramus (201) 262-5151
www.njcm.com

With over thirty exhibits in 15,000 square feet, this museum will keep your little ones busy no matter what their interests or ages. Exhibits include the "Baby Nook, "Housekeeping," and "Science and Technology." In the fire truck, your children can dress in real fire gear, sit in the truck and steer and ring the bell. In the "Kid-Sized Grocery" they can shop, fill their carts and check out at the register. At the "Kid-Sized Pizzeria" they can "cook" and serve everything from pizza to fish and broccoli. And in "The Medieval Castle" they can dress as kings, queens, knights and princesses.
Hours: October–April, weekdays 9 am–5 pm, weekends 10 am–6 pm; May–September, weekdays 9 am–5 pm, weekends 10 am–5 pm; closed Thanksgiving and Christmas Day **Admission:** $8 per person, free for children under 1 **What to Know Before You Go:** No strollers are permitted in the museum.

Savvy Savings

Check to see if your or your spouse's company participates in a corporate cultural savings program. You may be able to get in free at many museums zoos and other locations that require admission.

Theaters, Concerts & Children's Performances

By the time your child is 3 or 4, you'll probably have had it with "Sesame Street Live." The good news is he can now probably sit through a show, especially if it's one designed with kids in mind. There are an awful lot of choices available—whether you're looking for a production of a classic story, an original production, a puppet show or a kid's concert.

BRONXVILLE
The Corner Store
1428 Midland Ave., 2-J (914) 237-8680
www.thecornerstoredancecompany.org

Modern dance productions including live original music, storytelling, poetry, humor and a variety of musical instruments. Children participate from their seats, learning movements, words and songs. A different show is offered each year.
Cost: Varies
Ages: 3–12

Musical Adventures for Children
Concordia Conservatory, 171 White Plains Rd. (914) 395-4507

Series of three Saturday morning concerts for children.
Cost: $35 adults, $20 children (*for the series*)
Ages: 3–7

ELMSFORD
Westchester Broadway Theater
1 Broadway Plaza (914) 592-2222
www.broadwaytheatre.com

Unlike the performances for adults, there is no food service for Children's Theatre productions. Also, since seating is at tables, all tables are potentially shared tables. Recent productions have included "Charlie and the Chocolate Factory," "The Wizard of Oz" and "'Twas the Night Before Christmas."
Cost: Varies
Ages: Varies

IRVINGTON
Irvington Town Hall Theater
85 Main St. (914) 761-7463
This venue puts on tried-and-true shows as well as original productions. Recent shows include "The Life and Rhymes of Fiona Gander," "The Prince and the Pauper," and the "All-Star Broadway Holiday Concert."
Cost: Varies
Ages: Varies

MAMARONECK
Emelin Theater
153 Library Ln. (914) 698-0098
www.emelin.org

In addition to a repertoire of grown-up shows, the Emelin Theater offers a wide range of children's theater pieces. Recent shows include "Charlotte's Web," and "Alice in Wonderland." Performers include Raggs Kids Club and The Paper Bag Players. Most children's events are general admission, and people are seated on a first-come, first-served basis.
Cost: Varies
Ages: 3 and up

PLEASANTVILLE
Jacob Burns Film Center
364 Manville Rd. (914) 747-5555
www.burnsfilmcenter.org

Originally named The Rome Theater, this beautiful Spanish mission-style cinema, built in 1925, was one of the first movie theaters in Westchester County. It closed its doors in 1987 due to competition with neighboring multiplexes until a group, led by founder Stephen Apkon, bought it with hopes of restoring it to its former glory. The JBFC opened its doors to the public in June 2001 and has featured films ranging from human rights documentaries to Shakespeare. They also show classic films for kids like "The Wizard of Oz," "A Little Princess" and "Charlotte's Web."
Cost: Varies
Ages: Varies

PURCHASE
The Performing Arts Center
735 Anderson Hill Rd. (914) 251-6200
www.artscenter.org

A five-theater complex on the Purchase College campus.
Recent children's programming has included "Maurice
Sendak's Little Bear," "Zoppe Family Circus", "The Red
Balloon" and "The Giving Tree."
Cost: Varies
Ages: 3–9

SCARSDALE
Bendheim Performing Arts Center
JCC of Mid-Westchester, 999 Wilmot Rd. (914) 472-3300

In addition to grown-up shows, the Bendheim offers a
variety of children's performances. Recent shows include
"The Magic Land of Peter Pan" and "Mixed-Up Mother Goose."
Cost: Varies
Ages: Varies

TARRYTOWN
The Tarrytown Music Hall
13 Main St. (914) 631-3390
www.tarrytownmusichall.org

The Music Hall offers "Shows for Young Audiences on
Weekdays." Recent shows have included Judy Blume's
"Otherwise Known as Sheila The Great," "The Lion, The
Witch, and The Wardrobe" and "Bravo, Amelia Bedelia."
Cost: Varies
Ages: Varies

WHITE PLAINS
The Play Group Theatre
200 Hamilton Ave. #4B (914) 946-4433
www.playgroup.org

This children's theater produces shows by children, for
children in various area theaters. Recent shows include

"Charlotte's Web" and "The Sound of Music."
Cost: $15 adults, $10 children under 12
Ages: Varies

Westco Productions
9 Romar Ave. (914) 761-7463
www.westcoprods.com

Westco puts on three traditional holiday performances in November and December for kids: "Frosty the Snowman," "The Wizard of Oz," and a hospital tour of "The Frog Prince." The theater has recently expanded its scope to include other musical adaptations of well-known classics such as "The Diary of Anne Frank," "Hair," "Annie" and various Shakespeare plays. Shows are performed at venues like the Rochambeau School's theater at Westchester Broadway Theater and at the Irvington Town Hall. Westco also offers children's theater workshops: an introduction to theater for kids 3–4 *(with parent or caregiver)* and a workshop for kids 5–12 that culminates with the performance of a show.
Cost: Varies
Ages: 2–12

YORKTOWN
Yorktown Stage
Yorktown Community Cultural Center
1974 Commerce St. *(entrance off Veterans Rd.)*
(914) 962-0606
www.yorktownstage.com

Recent productions include "Annie," "The King and I," "The Nutcracker," and "Snow White."
Cost: Varies
Ages: Varies

MANHATTAN
13th Street Repertory Company
50 West 13th St. *(at 6th Ave.)* (212) 675-6677
www.13thstreetrep.org

Weekend performances of original children's shows. Recent

shows include "Rumple Who?" and "Wiseacre Farm."
Cost: $7 *(cash only, at box office)*
Ages: Varies

Literally Alive
(212) 866-5170
www.literallyalive.com

A theatrical production company that specializes in bringing classic children's literature to life on the stage through
music, art, dance, puppetry and storytelling. In addition to
the productions, families can participate in pre-show workshops. Recent productions include "Beauty and the Beast"
and "The Velveteen Rabbit," which were both performed at
the YWCA at 53rd St. & Lexington Ave.
Cost: Varies
Ages: Varies

The Little Orchestra Society
Avery Fisher Hall at Lincoln Center *(66th St. and Broadway)*
or The Kaye Playhouse at Hunter College *(695 Park Ave. at
68th St.)* (212) 971-9500
www.littleorchestra.org

107

Lolli-Pops concerts teach the ABCs of music, accompanied
by "Bow" the Panda, "Toot" the Bird, "Buzz" the Bee and
"Bang" the Lion, each representing a different section of
the orchestra. Happy Concerts for Young People produces
plays such as "Peter and the Wolf" and "Amahl and the
Night Visitors."
Cost: $99 for a Lolli-Pops 3-show subscription; $10-50 for
each Happy Concert
Ages: Lolli-Pops, 3–5; Happy Concerts, 6–12

Manhattan Children's Theater
380 Broadway at White St., 4th floor (212) 252-2840
www.manhattanchildrenstheatre.org

Weekend performances for kids and families. Recent shows
include "Riki-Tikki-Tavi," "Aesop's Fables" and "Alice in

Wonderland."
Cost: $12 adults, $10 children
Ages: Varies

New Victory Theater

209 W. 42nd St. *(just west of Broadway)* (212) 382-4000
www.newvictory.org

A beautifully restored landmark Broadway theater just for
kids, with afternoon, early evening and weekend perform-
ances. Recent shows include "A Year with Frog and Toad,"
"The New Shanghai Circus," and "Twinkle Twinkle Little
Fish."
Cost: $7–28 members, $10–40 non-members; membership is
automatic when you order tickets to three or more shows.
Ages: Varies

Papageno Puppet Theater

The Little Theater at the West End
2911 Broadway *(111th St.)* (212) 874-3297

Various children's shows *(pizza not included!)*.
Cost: $8
Ages: 0–10

Paper Bag Players

225 W. 99th St. (212) 663-0390
www.thepaperbagplayers.org

Original theater for children performed at The Kaye
Playhouse at Hunter College. Performances are on week-
ends, January–March.
Cost: $20–25
Ages: 4–9

Vital Theatre Company

432 West 42nd St. (212) 268-2040
www.vitaltheatre.org

Original children's theatre at weekend matinee performances.

Recent shows include "Animal of the Year" and "History Time Henry."
Cost: $14 per ticket, $40 for a Family Pass *(4 tickets you can use at multiple performances)*
Ages: Varies

CONNECTICUT
Quick Center for the Arts
Fairfield University, 1073 N. Benson Rd., Fairfield
(203) 254-4190
www.fairfield.edu/quick/quick.htm

Recent shows for children include "Red Riding Hood," "Jack and the Beanstalk," "The Pied Piper," and "Just So Stories."
Cost: $12 adults, $10 children
Ages: Varies

Rich Forum
263 Tresser Blvd., Stamford (203) 325-4466
www.onlyatsca.com

In addition to old favorites like "The Nutcracker," the Forum has special shows such as "My First Orchestra Concert," in which the music director of the Stamford Symphony Orchestra introduces kids to classical music.
Cost: Varies
Ages: Varies

Stamford Theater Works/Purple Cow Children's Theater
200 Strawberry Hill Ave., Stamford (203) 359-4414
www.stamfordtheatreworks.org

Children's shows are performed May through July and during the winter holiday season. Performances include stories, music, dance, puppetry, magic and lots of audience participation.
Cost: Varies
Ages: 3–8

PUTNAM COUNTY
Hudson Valley Shakespeare Festival
Boscobel Restoration, Rte. 9D, Garrison (845) 265-7858
www.hvshakespeare.org

An energetic, inventive cast performs Shakespeare under a
big yellow-and-white striped tent on the grounds of this
historic house museum. Productions are usually comedies
and are extremely accessible and entertaining, even for
young children. HVSF performs June-August. You can picnic
on the grounds before the show; either bring your own or
order one though the box office at (845) 265-9575.
Cost: $20-35 per ticket, depending on performance
Ages: Newborn and up

Savvy Suggestions

Wonderful Winter Excursions
* See the Holiday Train Show at the New York Botanical
  Garden in the Bronx
* Visit the festive holiday window displays of the big department
  stores in New York City.
* Take a pre-bedtime trip to The Bronx Zoo Holiday Lights
  event, which features lighted sculptures, ice carving
  demonstrations, and costumed characters.
* Go to the Palisades Center for hours of food, fun and games.
* Take a train ride into Grand Central Station for a fun
  indoor exploration.

Family Fun

Pools & Beaches
Miniature Golf
Apple-Picking & Pumpkin Patches
Zoos & Farms
Aquariums
Ice-Skating
Bowling

Here's the stuff you really moved to Westchester for. Things that make your city friends green with envy *(that is, in addition to not having to cram everything you own into two tiny closets)*. Pools, beaches and miniature golf in the summer. Picking your own apples and pumpkins in the fall. And, in the winter, lots of choices when it comes to indoor fun, like ice-skating and bowling. This is what suburbia is all about.

Pools & Beaches

When the temperature heats up, it's time to head for the water. In addition to cooling you down, the pools and beaches also offer entertainment to bring out the kid in anyone. At some of these places summertime fun even includes giant pool toys, face painting and deejay music. While there are plenty of municipal swimming pools in Westchester, most are restricted to town or village residents. We've listed them here for your information; check your local recreation department for hours and opening and closing dates.

Fortunately, there is a state park in Westchester with swimming facilities, and the Westchester County Parks system has four beaches and five pools available to all county residents. Most require a Westchester County Park Pass, which is available at many of the county park information centers, as well as at the Westchester County Center *(in White Plains)* and the Westchester County Parks Department *(in Mt. Kisco).* They cost $40 and are good for up to three years. Each pass allows free admission to county-owned park facilities for the pass holder and up to two guests; children under 12 are also admitted for free. With a pass you get to use all county-owned park facilities and you also get some discounts in user and parking fees. For more information, call the Parks Department at **(914) 864-PARK** or visit:

www.westchestergov.com/parks.

Hours at all county swimming areas are 10 am–6:30 pm, but opening and closing dates vary. For kids over 3, there are summer "Learn-to-Swim" classes at Sprain Ridge, Saxon Woods, and Tibbetts Brook *(children 3–5 must be accompanied by an adult).* Registration is required; for more information, call (914) 864-7056.

ARDSLEY
Anthony F. Veteran Park *(11 Olympic Ln.)*

BEDFORD
Bedford Hills Park *(Haines Rd.)*

Bedford Memorial Park *(Greenwich Rd., Bedford Village)*

Katonah Memorial Park *(North St., Katonah)*

BRIARCLIFF MANOR
Law Memorial Park *(Pleasantville Rd.)*

BUCHANAN
Recreation Site (West Ave.)

CORTLANDT
Charles J. Cook Recreation Center *(Furnace Dock Rd.)*

Sprout Brook Park *(Sprout Brook Rd.)*

CROTON-ON-HUDSON
Croton Point Park Beach *(Croton Point Ave.)*—County Park, no pass required; open weekends and holidays only

DOBBS FERRY
Gould Park *(Ashford Ave.)*

Memorial Park *(Palisade St.)*

ELMSFORD
Massaro Park *(50 Cabot Ave.)*

HARRISON
Bernie Guagnini Brentwood Park *(Webster Ave.)*

John Passidomo Veteran Park *(Lake St., W. Harrison)*

LEWISBORO
Town Park *(Rte. 35, South Salem)*

MAMARONECK
Hommocks Park Ice Rink & Swimming Pool Complex *(Hommocks Rd. & Rte. 1)*

MOUNT VERNON
Willson's Woods Park *(E. Lincoln Ave.)*
County Park Pass required; Westchester residents only

NEW ROCHELLE
Flower's Park/City Park *(City Park Rd., off Fifth Ave.)*

Glen Island Park Beach *(Pelham Rd.)*
County Park Pass required; Westchester residents only

Hudson Park *(Hudson Park Rd., off Pelham Rd.)*

Lincoln Park *(Lincoln Ave.)*

NORTH SALEM
Spruce Lake at Mountain Lakes Park *(Hawley Rd.)*
County Park, no pass required; open weekends and holidays only

113

PLEASANTVILLE
Nannahagen Park *(Lake St.)*

POUND RIDGE
Town Park *(Rte. 137)*

RYE
Playland *(Playland Parkway) (See Chapter 1 for more information)*— County Park, no pass required

(See Chapter 1 for more information)

Oakland Beach *(Dearborn & Forest)*

SCARSDALE
Municipal Pool *(Mamaroneck Rd.)*

WHITE PLAINS
Church Street School *(Church St.)*

Gardella Park *(Ferris & Park Aves.)*

Kittrell Park *(Bank St. & Fisher Ave.)*

Post Road School *(Post Rd.)*

Saxon Woods Park *(Mamaroneck Ave.)*
County Park Pass required for swimming

YONKERS
Sprain Ridge Park *(Jackson Ave.)*
County Park Pass required

Tibbetts Brook Park *(Midland Ave.)*
County Park Pass required; Westchester residents only

YORKTOWN
Franklin D. Roosevelt State Park *(2957 Crompond Rd.)*

Junior Lake Park *(Edgewater St., Yorktown Heights)*

Savvy Suggestion

"Twilight Swim," from 4 pm until closing, offers reduced admission fees at all county swimming areas, so that residents who work during the day have an opportunity to enjoy the swimming facilities.

Shrub Oak Park *(Sunnyside St., off of Rte. 6, Shrub Oak)*

Sparkle Lake *(Granite Springs Rd., Yorktown Heights)*

Savvy Suggestion

Delight your child with a train ride. Pick a destination on your local train route that you'd both like to explore. Most towns have plenty of stores, casual restaurants and diners and places of interest near the train station.

Miniature Golf

We're not sure if this is what "tilting at windmills" means, but it's probably the closest most of us are ever going to get to sinking a hole in one. Miniature golf is a great activity for kids as young as 2 or 3, and most grown-ups love it too. Most of these courses are open seasonally, so be sure to check with them before heading out.

ELMSFORD
Golden Bear Golf Center
300 Waterside Dr. (914) 592-1666

Cost: $7 adults, $5.50 children
Hours: Weekdays 8 am–10 pm, weekends 7 am–11 pm

MOHEGAN LAKE
Family Golf Center at Yorktown
2710 Lexington Ave. (914) 526-8337

Cost: $5 adults, $4 children
Hours: April–October, daily 8 am–8 pm; November–May, weekdays 9 am–8 pm, weekends 8 am–8 pm

NEW ROCHELLE
Glen Island Park
Pelham Rd. (914) 813-6720/-6721

Cost: $3 adults, $2 children; County Park Pass required for parking.
Hours: Memorial Day–Labor Day, 12–6 pm

RYE
Playland
Playland Parkway (914) 813-7000
www.ryeplayland.org

Cost: $3.50 per person
Hours: Daily 10 am until one hour before park closing

WHITE PLAINS
Saxon Woods Park
Mamaroneck Ave. (914) 995-4480/-4481

Cost: $3 adults, $2 children
Hours: Sunday–Thursday 12–8 pm, Friday–Saturday 12–9 pm

YONKERS
Tibbetts Brook Park
Midland Ave. (914) 231-2865

Cost: $3 adults, $2 children
Hours: Daily 11 am–7 pm

Apple-Picking & Pumpkin Patches

There's really nothing like a cup of fresh apple cider on a beautiful, sunny fall day with fresh air and colorful foliage. Many of the orchards and farms listed here have farm stands featuring their own products, including produce, cider, doughnuts, pies, fresh breads, maple syrup, fudge and various crafts and gift items. Most of them have great fall activities for the kids. After a fun day outdoors, you can return home and make a wonderful apple crisp or pie from your just-picked apples.

There are only three such farms in Westchester County, so we've included spots in Dutchess and Orange Counties, along with a few in Connecticut. In season, Westchester farms are often swarming on weekends; the farther you travel, the more you'll avoid the crowds *(and you'll also have a better pick of produce!).*

But don't limit your farm visits to autumn—a number of these spots offer fun for other seasons, including pick-your-own berries, peaches and flowers in spring and summer, and choose-your-own Christmas trees in the winter. Some have barnyard animals or zoos, playgrounds and other attractions. Orchards and farms are open seasonally and hours vary; call for more information.

117

WESTCHESTER

GRANITE SPRINGS
Stuart's Fruit Farm
Granite Springs Rd. (914) 245-2784
www.farmy.com/stuartsfarm.html

Here you can pick your own pumpkins as well as twenty
varieties of apples.

NORTH SALEM
Outhouse Orchards
Hardscrabble Rd. (914) 277-3188

Pick-your-own apples. They have a small zoo of geese,
ducks, goats, chickens and rabbits. On fall weekends, they
have events such as pony rides, face painting and hayrides.

YORKTOWN
Wilkens Fruit Farm
1335 White Hill Rd. (914) 245-5111
www.wilkensfarm.com

Pick-your-own apples, raspberries and pumpkins, as well as
several acres of "Choose-n-Cut Christmas Trees." A wagon
ride takes you to and from the orchard.

CONNECTICUT

BETHEL
Blue Jay Orchards
125 Plumtree Rd. (203) 748-0119
www.bluejayorchards.com

Pick-your-own apples, pears, peaches and pumpkins. In
September and October there are hayrides and a maze.

EASTON
Silverman's Farm
451 Sports Hill Rd. (203) 261-3306
www.silvermansfarm.com

Pick-your-own apples, peaches, plums, nectarines, flowers and pumpkins. There is a cider mill, where you can watch apple cider being made, and an animal farm with buffalo, llamas, sheep, pigs, exotic birds and more. In the fall, there are tractor rides and hayrides.

Savvy Suggestion

Easy Apple Crisp
Peel and thin-slice ten MacIntosh apples. Layer them ¾ of the way up a baking dish (with or without pie crust). Pour ½ cup apple juice over the apples.
Combine ¾ cup flour, ¾ cup brown sugar and 1 tsp. cinnamon. Cut in one stick of butter or margarine. Sprinkle mixture over the apples and pat down. Bake in a preheated 325° F oven for 45 minutes.

119

REDDING
Warrup's Farm
51 John Reed Rd. (203) 938-9403
www.localharvest.org/farms/m4687

Pick-your-own peaches, pumpkins, vegetables, flowers and herbs. There are also maple syrup demonstrations, barnyard animals and, in season, hayrides.

SHELTON
Jones Family Farms
266 Israel Hill Rd. (203) 939-8425
www.jonesfamilyfarm.com

Pick-your-own strawberries, blueberries and pumpkins, and choose-your-own Christmas trees. In the fall, there are hayrides and horse-drawn wagon rides.

DUTCHESS COUNTY

HOPEWELL JUNCTION
Keepsake Orchards
9 Fishkill Farms Rd. (845) 897-2266
www.keepsakeorchards.com

Pick-your-own apples, strawberries, raspberries, blackberries, blueberries, peaches, cherries and pumpkins. There is also a petting zoo and seasonal activities, including hayrides, live music and live wood-carving demonstrations.

PAWLING
Dykeman's Farm
231 West Dover Rd. (845) 832-6068
www.bestcorn.com

Pick-your-own raspberries, apples, flowers, winter squash, pumpkins and a wide variety of other vegetables, including tomatoes and peppers. During pumpkin season, there are hayrides, refreshments, face painting and other events.

POUGHQUAG
Barton Orchards
63 Apple Tree Ln. (845) 227-2306
www.bartonorchards.com

Pick-your-own strawberries, raspberries, blueberries, peaches, apples and pumpkins. There's also a petting zoo and a playground. In the fall, enjoy weekend Harvest Festivals, with live entertainment, pony rides, hayrides and a corn maze.

ORANGE COUNTY

WARWICK
Applewood Orchards & Winery
82 Four Corners Rd. (845) 986-1684
www.applewoodorchards.com

Pick-your-own apples and pumpkins. In addition to the orchards and winery, there are barnyard animals, including ducks, horses, bunnies and sheep. In the fall, there are hayrides, music and puppet shows.

Pennings Farm Market
161 Rte. 94 S. (845) 986-1059
www.penningsfarmmarket.com

Pick-your-own apples. Pennings also features "Barnyard Buddies Feeding Corral," "Pennings Express 'Play-Train'," and a playground. In season, there are hayrides, a haunted house, live music, story telling, pony rides and other activities.

121

Zoos & Farms

Nothing fascinates preschoolers and young children like a visit with our furry friends—that's the theory at least. Laura's son was far more interested in the school buses in the parking lot than in the rare and exotic animals inside the zoo. Honestly, for the first few years of your children's lives, you should probably look at trips to a zoo or farm as something fun and different for you, not them. Your children's ability to appreciate their surroundings will eventually follow.

SLEEPY HOLLOW
Philipsburgh Manor
Rte. 9 (914) 631-3992
www.hudsonvalley.org/web/phil-main.html

This stone manor house was once owned by the Philips family, which was one of the wealthiest in New York and one of the largest slaveholders in the area. Now a living history museum, the estate features a 1680's Manor House, a working eighteenth-century barn and water-powered grist mill, and a reconstructed tenant farmhouse. The grounds are home to historic breeds of cattle, sheep and chickens. There are hands-on exhibits and tours featuring scripted vignettes. Picnic facilities overlook the millpond and the Greenhouse Café is open May–October. Tours of Kykuit, the Rockefeller Estate, leave from here, but they're not appropriate for children under 10.

Hours: March weekends only, 10 am–4 pm; April–October, Wednesday–Monday 10 am–5 pm; November–December, Wednesday–Monday 10 am–4 pm

Admission: $9 adults, $5 children 5–17, free for children under 5

SOMERS
Muscoot Farm
Rte. 100 (914) 864-7282
www.co.westchester.ny.us/parks

Owned by Westchester County, Muscoot Farm covers 777 acres. Visitors can walk through the Dairy Barn, Milk House, Ice House, Blacksmith Shop and several other barns and buildings. There are more than seven miles of hiking trails; trail maps are available in the reception center. Popular annual events for families include "Meet the Baby Animals," "Tractor Day" and pumpkin picking. Muscoot also offers other events, as well as a variety of Saturday workshops throughout the year. Hayrides are offered April–October on Sunday afternoons, weather permitting.

Hours: Open daily 10 am–4 pm, Open weekends Memorial Day through Labor Day 10 am-5 pm.

Cost: Hayrides—$2 per person

What to Know Before You Go: On May–October weekends a variety of foods and beverages are available. Visitors are not allowed to pet or feed the farm animals. Dogs are not allowed.

YONKERS
Stew Leonard's
1 Stew Leonards Dr. (914) 375-4700
www.stewleonards.com

Hailed as the "Disneyland of Dairy Stores" by the *New York Times*, Stew Leonard's has a petting and feeding zoo, as well as animatronics throughout the store. A big plus: you can get your shopping done at the same time! They also have two locations in Connecticut.
Hours: Daily 8 am–10 pm
Cost: Free

MANHATTAN & THE BRONX
Bronx Zoo
Fordham Rd. & Bronx River Parkway *(Exit 6)*, Bronx
(718) 367-1010
www.wcs.org/home/zoos/bronxzoo

The largest metropolitan zoo in the nation, this zoo has more than 6,000 animals. The wonderful exhibits, include the new Congo Gorilla Forest, where you can get nose-to-nose with Western lowland gorillas, JungleWorld, and the Himalayan Highlands. The Children's Zoo has a petting and feeding zoo for the little ones, and the zoo offers other programs for families, preschoolers and older kids *(additional fees apply).* Food is available at several cafes and snack stands, some with seating. One last thing: the Zoo is massive, so even if you have a child who loves to walk, it's a good idea to bring or rent a stroller.
Hours: April–October, weekdays 10 am–5 pm, weekends and holidays 10 am–5:30 pm; November–March, daily 10:30 am–4:30 pm
Admission: $11 adults, $6 children 2–12, free for children under 2; free on Wednesday *(but the suggested donation is the same as the general admission price);* Children's Zoo—$2 per person; parking—$7
What to Know Before You Go: For the Children's Zoo, go to Parking Lot C *(Exit #7 off the Bronx River Parkway).* Additional entry fees apply for some exhibits, such as the Congo Gorilla Forest. Strollers are available for daily rental *($6 for a single, $10 for a double).* Strollers must be collapsed on rides and checked or left outside at some exhibits.

Central Park Zoo

830 Fifth Ave., New York (212) 439-6500
www.wcs.org/home/zoos/centralpark

Right in the middle of Manhattan, you can visit a rain forest and an Antarctic habitat, and see more than 1,400 animals. The new Tisch Children's Zoo lets kids see animals up close. And don't forget the sea lion feedings! The zoo also offers a variety of education classes, programs and special events. Snacks and beverages are available in The Café.

Hours: April–October, weekdays 10 am–5 pm, weekends and holidays 10 am–5:30 pm; November–March, daily 10:30 am–4:30 pm

Admission: $3.50 adults, $0.50 children 3–12, free for children under 3

What to Know Before You Go: Enter Central Park at 65th St. & 5th Ave. and walk south one block. Other attractions within walking distance are Wollman Rink, a little further west in Central Park, and the FAO Schwartz flagship store at 59th St. & 5th Ave.

CONNECTICUT
Beardsley Zoo

1875 Noble Ave., Bridgeport (203) 394-6565
www.beardsleyzoo.org

Located on fifty-two acres of Beardsley Park, this zoo has more than 300 animals, including some endangered species. Exhibits include: a South American rainforest, a New England Farmyard including goats, cows, pigs and sheep, and a Victorian Carousel Museum with restored antique horses and rides. There is a restaurant, a snack bar and a picnic grove.

Hours: Daily 9 am–4 pm; closed Thanksgiving, Christmas Day and New Year's Day; New World Tropics Building—daily 10:30 am–3:30 pm; Carousel Museum—seasonally 10:30 am–4 pm

Admission: $7 adults, $5 children 3–11, free for children under 3

Heckscher Farm at Stamford Museum & Nature Center

39 Scofieldtown Rd., Stamford (203) 322-1646

www.stamfordmuseum.org/farm.html

This traditional working farm encompasses ten acres, with pigs, cows, goats, chickens and more. Walkways are paved, so strollers have easy access. Special seasonal events include spring planting, summer picking, fall apple cidering and winter crafts. A big draw: Nature's Playground, where kids can scale a spider's web, zoom down an otter slide or climb into a hawk's nest to survey their territory. The playground also has a picnic area.

Hours: Heckscher Farm—daily 9 am–4 pm; Nature's Playground—daily 9 am–5 pm; closed July 4th, Thanksgiving, Christmas Day and New Year's Day.

Admission: $6 adults; $5 children 3–14; free for children under 3 and for members

What to Know Before You Go: Visit from 10 am–noon or 3–5 pm to interact with the farm staff as they do their chores: feeding the animals, cleaning the barns, milking cows or goats, or collecting eggs.

Aquariums

Like children's museums, aquariums aren't very common in Westchester proper. Luckily for us, we are well-situated to take advantage of two fabulous aquariums nearby. As with other attractions, they tend to get very busy on the weekends, particularly in the winter; getting there when they open is often a good bet. However, if you want to see the animals eat, call ahead for feeding times and schedule your visit that way. These shows can also get very crowded, so try to get there early to get situated. Depending on your child, you might want to bring something to distract them while you're waiting for the show to start—perhaps a book, a small toy or a snack *(we're thinking Goldfish crackers)*.

BROOKLYN
New York Aquarium
Surf Ave. & W. 8th St. (718) 265-FISH
www.wcs.org/home/zoos/nyaquarium

Exhibits include two touch tanks with sea stars and horse-shoe crabs, a seahorse exhibit and a dolphin aquatheater *(May–October)*. The aquarium also offers a variety of educational programs and other public events.
Hours: April-May, weekdays 10 am–5 pm, weekends and holidays 10 am–5:30 pm; May- September, weekdays 10 am-6pm, weekends and holidays 10 am–7 pm; September-October weekdays 10 am–5 pm, weekends and holidays 10 am–5:30 pm
Admission: $11 adults, $7 children 2–12; $7 parking
What to Know Before You Go: There is an indoor cafeteria with an ocean view, and an outdoor snack bar. Picnic tables are also available.

CONNECTICUT
Maritime Aquarium at Norwalk
10 N. Water St., Norwalk (203) 852-0700
www.maritimeaquarium.org

A small, "doable" aquarium, featuring more than 1,000 marine animals native to the Long Island Sound and its watershed. Exhibits include an indoor-outdoor tank for harbor seals; the 110,000-gallon "Open Ocean" tank, with nine-foot sharks, bluefish, striped bass, rays and other creatures; the sea turtle tank; and the Touch Tank, with sea stars, crabs, and other tidal creatures. In "Ocean Playspace," kids up to age 5 can enjoy soft play structures, a Titanic play ship, and dressing up with life jackets, fins and flippers. There are also other special exhibits and an IMAX theater.
Hours: September–June, daily 10 am –5 pm; July–August, daily 10 am–6 pm; closed Thanksgiving and Christmas Day
Admission: $9.25 adults, $7.50 children 2–12
What to Know Before You Go: Seal feedings are at 11:45 am, 1:45 pm and 3:45 pm daily. There are good food stands and cafés inside. No outside food or drink is allowed. The aquarium is located in the historic waterfront neighborhood of South Norwalk ("SoNo"), which has lots of boutiques, eclectic shops, delis and restaurants.

Ice-Skating

We know a boy who was on ice skates by the age of three. At the ripe old age of seven, he now plays hockey on a prestigious traveling team. For all you parents out there who have dreams of one day seeing your little ones in an "Ice Spectacular" or being recruited by the NHL, you'll be glad to know that there are many indoor ice-skating rinks throughout Westchester. Here's one thing to consider before you choose ice-skating as your child's "thing": most leagues practice early and often. Brace yourself for 5:30 am departures and weekend trips to the picturesque likes of Hoboken, New Jersey. But skating is great fun and something that can be enjoyed year-round.

The ice rinks listed below are indoors; for outdoor ice-skating locations, check out our listings in Chapter 1 under "Community Playgrounds" and "County & State Parks." Outdoor facilities are, of course, seasonal, as are some of the indoor facilities. Call for specific opening and closing information, since many rinks open and close throughout the day and have specific times set aside for lessons, hockey clubs and free skate/public skating sessions. All of the facilities listed here offer figure skating, hockey, free skate and lessons. Some have skate rental, and most offer birthday parties.

ELMSFORD
Westchester Skating Academy
91 Fairview Park Dr. (914) 347-8232
www.skatewsa.com
Cost: $8.50 adults, $7.50 children

KATONAH
Harvey School Rink
260 Jay St. *(Rte. 22)* (914) 232-3618
Cost: $5 per half hour

LARCHMONT
Hommocks Park Ice Rink
Boston Post Rd. & Weaver St. (914) 834-3164
Cost: $6 adults, $5 children *(non-residents);* $4 adults, $3.50 children *(Mamaroneck residents)*

MOUNT VERNON
The Ice Hutch
655 Garden Ave. (914) 699-6787
Cost: $6 per person

NEW ROCHELLE
New Roc Ice at New Roc City
New Roc City,
33 LeCount Pl. *(Exit 16 off I-95)* (914) 637-7575
www.newroccity.com/new_roc_ice.htm
Cost: $8 per person

RYE
Playland Ice Casino
Playland Parkway (914) 813-7010
www.ryeplayland.org
Cost: $6 adults, $4 children under 12

YONKERS
Edward J. Murray Memorial Skating Center
348 Tuckahoe Rd. (914) 377-6469
Cost: $5 adults, $3.50 children

CONNECTICUT
Stamford Twin Rinks
1063 Hope St., Stamford
(203) 968-9000
www.icecenter.com
Cost: $7 adults, $5 children
12 and under

ROCKLAND COUNTY
Palisades Center Ice Rink
1000 Palisades Center Dr.
(4th floor, above Filene's),
West Nyack (845) 353-4855
www.palice.com
Cost: $7 adults, $5 children

Savvy Suggestion

Here's what to do when your child outgrows his ice skates in just one season: trade them in towards a new pair of skates for next year at Bob Peck's Skate and Sport Shop, 31 Lake St., 2nd floor, White Plains, (914) 949-0579. The trade-in value is generally $15-35, depending on the condition of the skates.

Bowling

Like miniature golf, you might not consider bowling to be an activity for the little ones, but the truth is, once they can walk well, they can bowl. And with a little luck *(and a little help)*, they'll be able to propel the ball down the lane and knock down a few pins—something that is sure to fill them with glee and delight.

All of the bowling centers listed below have bumpers for small children. Many offer other activities, such as video games and billiards, and most have a snack bar or restaurant. League play—yes, teams of people in kitschy shirts—takes up most lanes on evenings and weekends, so be sure to call for hours and availability before you go.

Savvy Suggestion

Bowl-At-Home
Decorate empty soda bottles or cardboard paper towel tubes with paint, markers or stickers and arrange them as "bowling pins." You and your child can "bowl" by rolling or tossing a rolled-up pair of socks or a small, soft ball at the "pins."

129

JEFFERSON VALLEY
Jefferson Valley Bowl
3699 Hill Blvd. (914) 245-7771

Twenty-four lanes, a snack bar, video games, billiards, foosball and air hockey.
Cost: Weekdays $3.25 per person, evenings and weekends $4 per person

NEW ROCHELLE
New Roc 'n Bowl
New Roc City, 33 LeCount Pl. *(Exit 16 off I-95)* (914) 637-7575
www.newroccity.com/new_roc_bowl.htm

In addition to seventeen lanes of bowling, this site has glow-in-the-dark bowling, air hockey, virtual bowling, foosball and a deejay on Friday and Saturday nights.
Cost: $3-7 per game, depending on day of week and time of day.

PEEKSKILL
Cortlandt Lanes
2292 Crompond Rd. (914) 737-4550

Thirty-eight lanes, a restaurant, a bar and a snack bar.
Cost: Weekdays $4 per person, evenings and weekends
$4.50 per person

WHITE PLAINS
AMF White Plains Lanes
47 Tarrytown Rd. (914) 948-2677
www.amfcenters.com

Fifty-six lanes, a snack bar and video games.
Cost: Weekdays $5.50 per person, evenings and weekends
$6.50 per person

YONKERS
Cross County Lanes
790 Yonkers Ave.
(914) 423-2088

Twenty lanes, a bar, a snack
bar and video games.
Cost: Weekdays $3.50
adults, $2.50 children;
evenings and weekends $4.75
per person

Homefield Bowl
938 Saw Mill River Rd.
(914) 969-5592

Thirty-two lanes, a bar, a snack bar and video games.
Cost: Weekdays $4.75 per person; weekends $5.50 per person

CONNECTICUT
Bowlarama III
109 Hamilton Ave., Stamford (203) 323-1041

Twenty lanes, a snack bar and video games.
Cost: $5 per person

Savvy Superlatives

**Our Seasonal Favorites
for a Family Saturday**
Winter: A trip to
Maritime Aquarium at
Norwalk
Spring: "Meet the Baby
Animals" at Muscoot Farm
Summer: Swimming
and miniature golf at
Saxon Woods
Fall: Apple-picking at
any area orchard

Whining & Dining

Some Suggestions for Eating Out with Your Child

"Where is the section on family-friendly restaurants?" you may be asking. Well, first let's define the term "family-friendly." Do you mean the hostess won't give you the hairy eyeball when you request a highchair? Do you mean you can leave a pile of half-eaten french fries and Cheerios under your child's seat without fear of being banned for life? Or do you mean that the other diners in the restaurant won't cluck their tongues and roll their eyes when you are seated next to them? The truth is that any and all of these things can happen anyplace from the most casual to the most formal restaurant.

Of course, parents eat out with their children all the time, so we wanted to offer some tips on making it a pleasant experience for everyone. Before you go, ask yourself a few questions.

131

What is my child's temperament?

Can he sit quietly playing with a spoon for hours or will he squirm and scream after five minutes of restricted mobility? Temperament is important, and age has a lot to do with it. Once, Betsy was sitting in a restaurant with her screaming eighteen-month-old. A woman sitting at the next table looked over and smiled sympathetically. "Now I remember why I don't do this often," Betsy said, feeling miserable. "Oh, I've been taking Tyler to restaurants since she was born," the mother responded. "I wanted her to get used to them." It turned out Tyler was only nine months old—a much easier age for restaurant visits *(assuming they're not walking yet!).* "Just wait six months," Betsy said. It's a great idea to try to get your child used to restaurants, but we're not convinced it really works. Although Laura has a friend who swears that her impeccable table manners are the result of frequent childhood visits to the likes of Le Cirque, at a certain age many kids discover that crawling under the table is much more interesting than sitting at it. Only you know how much "table time" your child can tolerate. Do yourself and every diner a favor: follow your kid's lead.

What is the purpose of this meal?

Are you trying to catch up with a girlfriend you haven't seen since you had the baby? Are you attempting to have a much-needed romantic night out with your husband? Do you just want to get out of the house? Whatever the situation, know that if you bring your child, at a certain point you may be required to give the little one sitting next to you more attention than the grown-up seated across from you. Take Betsy's thirtieth birthday, for example. A close friend took her to lunch at the restaurant in the upscale store Barney's. As soon as the food arrived they had to send it back to be wrapped up "to go," then ate their meal in the bathroom so that her friend could comfortably breastfeed.

If you really want to be able to relax and enjoy your friend's company, try doing it over coffee. That way, no one is waiting for a waitress to reappear and if you have to leave abruptly you haven't ruined a perfectly good meal. The less pressure you put on yourself and your child, the more relaxed you'll be.

If you're trying to reconnect with your spouse over a nice meal, we strongly suggest that you take up your parents or in-laws on their offer to baby-sit. If you don't have any friends or family nearby, bite the bullet and hire someone for a few hours. *(To find a baby-sitter, check out our suggestions in Chapter 8.)* Skipping dessert or choosing a slightly less expensive place will make the cost of the baby-sitter easier to swallow.

What is my humiliation threshold?

For some parents, that hairy eyeball will have them running for the parking lot, while others will casually step over the pile of discarded bits of food and sugar packets on the floor with nary a care. Ask yourself—honestly—how much you can take. No one wants to ruin another person's dinner, but we all cry "uncle" at different points. If you eat at restaurants that are obviously family-friendly (*lots of highchairs, free crayons and coloring books, and a specific children's menu*), it will certainly be easier to hold your head high if your child makes a fuss, a mess or a dirty diaper. We've listed some of our favorite family-friendly restaurants at this end of the chapter.

Laura also has a trusty method for managing the rough spots: she thinks of her cousin, who spent every Thanksgiving crawling under the table rather than sitting at it. He grew up to become a director of communications at The White House. In other words, your child's early table behavior is not an indicator of his or her future potential—nor is it an indicator of your parenting skills. Think about that when the stares start.

OK, ready to go out to eat? Here are a few tips to chew on:

Choose wisely. Yes, you can get nasty, withering looks at a diner just as easily as you can at an exclusive French restaurant, but somehow it's easier to deal with them when you're in jeans rather than formalwear and the entrees cost less than $25. If your child spills strained peas all over the tray at a fast-food restaurant, it's really no big deal. Old-fashioned diners—which are ubiquitous in Westchester—generally have speedy service and a high tolerance for messiness, which is critical when you venture out with young children.

Go at off-hours. When the restaurant is slower, the service is faster. Go to dinner at 5 or 5:30 pm, before the place fills up. This is a great end-of-the-day activity, leaving you only bath and bedtime to deal with when you get home.

Line up your requests like dominoes. Order something for your child as soon as you are seated—that plate of french fries may buy you valuable time as you wait for the rest of the food to arrive. Ask for the check before you're ready for it, so you're not stuck searching for a waiter as your toddler—ready to go—dissolves into hysterics. If they require that you pay at the register (*which is always a little annoying*) it's helpful to have a few singles in your wallet for the tip so that you don't have to return to the table once you've packed up all your paraphernalia.

Savvy Suggestion

Get ready for takeoff at this unique eatery. Watch planes take off and land at the Skytop Restaurant in the Main Terminal of the Westchester Airport. Much better than "airplane food," the dishes here include lobsters flown in from Maine and homemade desserts.
Skytop Restaurant
I-684, exit 2, White Plains (914) 428-0251
Hours: Daily 11 am–9 pm
What to Know Before You Go: Don't forget to ask for a window table. And bring your parking slip to get it validated.

Don't forget your bag of tricks. Put in age-appropriate toys for your children like paper and crayons, matchbox cars or dolls, Legos, stickers and a small book or two. Add a few new things every now and again; not only will the toys occupy them before or after they've eaten, but they'll look forward to playing with toys that they don't see that often. Another benefit is that you'll always have the bag ready and waiting, saving you valuable time as you're trying to get out the door.

Be creative with your environment. Look around— kid-friendly activities may be right at your fingertips. Laura has kept Sam occupied until the food comes by building a house with sugar packets *(by the way, she says sugar substitutes work best),* identifying letters on the ketchup bottle, or counting the people in the restaurant.

B.Y.O. Always bring a stash of food you know your child will eat: Goldfish, cereal, yogurt, baby food, whatever. Even if your child is typically a really good eater, it never hurts to have a back-up plan just in case.

It may seem like eating out with children requires as much strategy as a military operation, but don't fret: like anything, it just takes a little practice. We believe in always setting yourself up for success. There is nothing better than the day you realize that eating out with your kids isn't just doable, but a lot of fun!

Savvy Superlatives

Our Favorite Family-Friendly Restaurants

* **Bellizzi** *(Pizza & play area)* 153 Main St., Mt. Kisco (914) 241-1200
* **Boxcar Cantina** *(Mexican)* 44 Old Field Point Rd., Greenwich, CT (203) 661-4774
* **California Pizza Kitchen** *(Pizza, pastas & salads)* 365 Central Park Ave., Scarsdale (914) 722-0600
* **Central Square Cafe** *(American)* 870 Central Park Ave., Scarsdale (914) 472-7828
* **City Limits Diner** *("Haute" diner)* 200 Central Ave., White Plains (914) 686-9000; Westchester Mall, 125 Westchester Ave., White Plains (914) 761-1111; 135 Harvard Ave., Stamford, CT (203) 348-7000
* **Ecco-La** *(Pizza & pasta)* 202 E. Hartsale Ave., Hartsdale (914) 472-5411
* **Sam's** *(Italian)* 128 Main St., Dobbs Ferry (914) 693-9724
* **Sports Page Pub** *(American, with dozens of TVs and a children's play area)* 1205 Mamaroneck Ave., White Plains (914) 761-6697

Desperately Seeking Mary Poppins

Day Care Centers
Nannies
Au Pairs
Baby-Sitters
Baby Nurses & Doulas
Background Checks & Nanny Cams
Employment Tax Services

Whether you are looking for someone to watch your child for forty hours a week or for four, the prospect of leaving your most precious possession in someone else's care can bring some parents to the brink of hysteria. There are so many questions. Nanny or day care? Where do I find a baby-sitter? How old should she be? DOES SHE HAVE A CRIMINAL HISTORY? Well, it's something every parent wonders about. How do you choose the right person or people to take care of your child?

We are experts only in the sense that we've both been through the process of hiring caregivers. Laura has had the same nanny since Sam was two-and-a-half-months old, while Betsy has had about as many nannies as Murphy Brown had secretaries. So here's what we've learned.

They're Out There—Be Patient

Don't panic. It's a big decision, and it can provoke a lot of anxiety. But there really is someone or someplace great out there that will fit *(most of)* your needs. Don't settle for a situation that won't work for you.

Write Up a Wish List

Take a few minutes to sit down and figure out what your needs really are. Do you need child care just a few hours a week, so you can make it to the gym or run errands that are decidedly more difficult with a child in tow? Do you want someone who will help out with housework? Cook? Do laundry? If you're looking for a full-time nanny, do you want her to live in or live out? Is cost a big issue?

Writing down a wish list will help considerably in your search. And try to be honest with yourself—you may love cooking, but after a really full day *(and possibly a commute home)* it might be nice to have dinner ready and waiting. And also try to think ahead—if you have an infant, while you're probably not concerned about toilet training yet, someday you will be. The rules or attitudes of the child care provider are important to know about ahead of time.

Narrowing Down Your Search

Once you've written your wish list, it should become more clear what type of situation will suit you best. In this chapter, we're going to cover five main areas of child care: **day care, nannies, au pairs, baby-sitters and nurses and doulas.** While we both ended up going the nanny route, we have friends who have used each of these options, so we'll give you the benefit of our collective experience.

We feel that no matter which child care option you choose, nothing beats word-of-mouth recommendations when it comes to finding a good person or place. So once you have an idea of what you're looking for, the first thing to do is ask your friends and neighbors. After you've done that, take a look at the suggestions below to help you find the right situation for you and your child.

Day Care Centers

Day care centers offer group care, and as a result are probably the most affordable route *(about $900–1200 per month)* if you're going to need your child looked after for many hours. Unfortunately, there are long waiting lists for many Westchester facilities, some as long as six months.

Location is certainly a primary consideration, as you'll probably want the center to be near your home or work for easier drop-off and pick-up. You'll also want to make sure that they have coverage for enough hours. Most day care centers that Laura looked at for Sam closed by 7 pm; she and her husband both work in New York City, and they weren't sure they'd be able to make it by closing time every night. In New York State, the teacher-to-child ratio is mandated, but some centers may exceed the State standards, so it's worthwhile to ask.

Some Other Things to Consider:

* Most importantly, do the children look happy? Are they having fun?
* Are the caregivers or teachers engaged and energetic? Are they caring and attentive, especially when children need help or attention?
* Does it feel safe? What are the rules for protecting your child?
* What are the facilities like? Do they have a good variety of toys, books and playthings? Is it bright and cheerful?
* How do they handle issues like separation, discipline and toilet training? What are their policies or rules?
* How do they handle emergencies? (If neither parent is working close by, you'll need to identify another contact person, just in case.)

Visit several centers, so you can gain some perspective and form a basis of comparison. Go when the kids are there, so you can see the center in action. Try to ask the same questions at each place you visit. And take your time—get a feel for the place. Usually the head of the center will give you a tour, discuss policies and rules, spend some time with you and answer your questions. If you want to talk further with the caregivers or teachers, hang around or come back when they aren't in session so they can give you their undivided attention. Ask all your questions, and trust your instincts. You'll know in your gut when you've found the right place.

For information on New York State licensing standards, click on **www.daycare.com/newyork**.

As you begin your search, check out the following resources.

Child Care Aware
(800) 424-2246
www.childcareaware.org

A nonprofit initiative that provides information and resources on child care.

Child Care Council of Westchester
470 Mamaroneck Ave., White Plains (914) 761-3456
www.childcarewestchester.org

A private, nonprofit organization that provides tons of resources and information on child care, as well as referrals in Westchester.

Daycareproviders.com
www.daycareproviders.com

Nationwide online child care directory *(providers pay a fee for listing),* plus information and links.

139

Medline Plus
www.nlm.nih.gov/medlineplus/childdaycare.html

Articles, research and information on child care. This website is run by the National Library of Medicine and the National Institutes of Health.

National Child Care Information Center
www.nccic.org

Department of Health and Human Services website with links and resources.

Nannies

Nannies generally work full-time, either living in or living out. There's a wide range of salaries on the market, but you should expect to pay around $350–600 per week. As we said before, the first place to start when looking for a nanny is to let everyone know that you're looking. Also, ask your friends' nannies if they know of anyone looking for a job—there's often a strong placement network among nannies. Once you've exhausted those two avenues, there are others to be explored.

Nanny Agencies

The theory here is that you will save time by having access to a prescreened group of women who are matched up with prospective employers according to their specific needs. (*Use your wish list to tell them what these needs are.*) Some agencies even specialize in placing women from a particular country. You can work with multiple agencies at the same time, but many agencies require you to pay a registration fee prior to receiving information about candidates. Most agencies have done preliminary background checks (*criminal record, driving violations*) that they will provide to you along with the basic application the candidates filled out. They usually have also done an initial reference check to see what kind of experience a former employer has had. In return for this "safety net" you can generally expect to pay a fee equal to one or two months of the nanny's salary or 10–12% of the annual salary as commission.

Agencies will usually give you only two or three candidates at a time to consider. The logic is that since they're sending you the applicants that most suit your needs, you won't have to interview lots and lots of people. As we suggested, be clear about what you're looking for in terms of days and hours per week, salary, duties, etc.

When you work with an agency, they might play an active role in salary negotiation, but often that is left up to the employer and the prospective employee. Usually, the agency will give you an idea of what pay range the candidate is looking for, or at least what she was making before.

When you've picked someone, agencies generally give you a trial period of about a week to see if your new nanny is going to work out before requiring you to pay the commission. If you're still not sure at the end of the week, then ask for a few extra days—the agency will probably agree. You are still responsible for paying the nanny a predetermined salary during the trial period.

Once you pay the commission, you'll have another one- or two-month trial period. If the candidate leaves or is fired within this period, most agencies agree to find you someone else for no additional charge. Certainly these services market themselves via their good reputation, but bear in mind that once they have your commission they may not be quite as motivated as they were the first time around. *(That said, one agency that Laura worked with said they would provide a prorated refund if they were unable to find a replacement.)*

Both of us have found nannies through agencies. As you know, Laura's is still with her. Betsy's lasted seven weeks and was never replaced by that agency *(which means she's out several thousand dollars)*. Laura worked with three agencies and felt the candidates to be of all-around higher quality than the others she met. On the other hand, Betsy felt that going through an agency didn't improve her odds of finding someone terrific and ultimately cost her far more. There's no right or wrong answer since obviously everyone's experience is different.

Classified Ads

If you ever start to doubt that the right person is out there, take a look at the classified listings in some of our recommended publications. There are literally dozens of women looking for positions and it only takes one to be your "Mary Poppins."

Both of us have placed ads in the *Irish Echo* and we each received more than 130 calls. Let your answering machine field the calls, or give your cell phone number only, and record a specific message asking candidates to leave their names, phone numbers and any other piece of pertinent information you may be looking for. *(For instance, "The job is live-out, Monday through Friday, from 7 am to 7 pm. If you are not able to work those hours, please do not leave a message.")* Many applicants will be weeded out by this process: Did they follow your instructions? Were they pleasant? Call the ones you are interested in back and conduct a phone interview. *(Don't forget to change your answering machine message back!)*

Sometimes a better option is to reply to an ad. Look for something special: Maybe she was with her previous family for eleven years. Or she can drive. Or she's CPR certified. Or, best of all, her previous or current employer placed the ad on her behalf to help her secure a good position. Generally this means they had an extremely positive experience and are giving up their nanny due to a change of circumstance *(they're moving, the children are older, etc.)*. Betsy found her current nanny this way and feels it's a great way to go. But act fast: these types of candidates will be scooped up quickly.

Another popular way of finding someone is to put up flyers at supermarkets, community centers, libraries, schools and other places that nannies may frequent. Often you can find flyers hung by people looking for positions *(again, some may be posted by current or previous employers)*.

Interview How-To

Conduct the initial interview by phone. Use this as an opportunity to let your gut be your guide. Is the person pleasant? Accommodating? Does she seem responsible? Is there any language barrier that may be a problem? Find out where she's worked and for how long. The age of the children she took care of. Whether or not she has children herself and how old they are. If she is not from this country you should find out if she is going to need to return home anytime in the near future *(say, within a year)*. You can start to form an overall impression about a candidate and decide whether or not you want to move to the next step and meet her in person. Make sure that she understands the parameters of the position and is able and willing to fulfill them. If there is any hesitation, consider that a red flag.

For candidates that interest you, get references. It can be helpful to check them prior to the actual interview. This is your chance to do the deep digging about someone else's experience. Of course, references are most likely going to give a glowing review, but you can ask former employers some pointed questions and compare them to answers you receive from the candidate, like: What were her responsibilities? What was her typical day like? How did your children interact with her? What did she do with them that you really liked? Did she do a thorough job or did you need to remind her to follow through on responsibilities? Did she call in sick often? Why did she leave? How were conflicts resolved? If you had to do it all over again, what would you look for that's different from this person? The more specific your questions are, the more helpful their answers will be. You can also use some of the information in your interview with a prospective nanny. For instance, "Wendy said that you occasionally prepared meals for the family. Is that something that you would do here?"

Still interested? Arrange to interview the candidate in person. If she's taking public transportation, it's customary to compensate her for the round-trip fare. Unless you are trying to replace a nanny currently in your house, it's helpful to conduct the interview in your home so you can pick up some useful insights and see how the candidate interacts with your child. Does she wash her hands before picking up the baby? Does she seem tentative or is she assertive? When Betsy asked one of her applicants if she had any questions after the interview the woman asked if her son had any allergies and at what point Betsy was planning on starting the potty training process. These and other thoughtful questions were geared towards being able to better take care of Simon. Not surprisingly, she got the job. When Laura met her nanny at the train station, the woman immediately put on her seatbelt, which none of the other candidates had done. At the house, she offered to change Sam's diaper, and did it lovingly and playfully *(and washed her hands before and after)*. That meant a lot.

Another good idea: make copies of your wish list, title it "Job Description," and give it to prospective candidates so they get a clear understanding of what you're looking for. It not only saves time during the interviewing process, but it can also be used for reference once you've hired someone.

You'll want to ask the candidate some of the same questions you asked her references. Some other things you might want to know: How would she comfort a crying baby. How flexible her schedule can be *(if she has small children, it may be less so)*. How she would handle a tantrum. What her attitudes are on discipline. Again, let your gut be your guide. If you get a good feeling for someone but are still unsure, ask her to come for a day as a trial *(you'll need to pay her for this)*. You can do the laundry, make phone calls and catch up on household chores while you observe her in action. And remember: good caregivers are pure gold. When you find someone terrific you'll want to hold onto her until your kid goes to college.

You can place an ad for a nanny *(or look for an ad)* in these publications:

Irish Echo
309 Fifth Ave., New York (212) 686-1266
www.irishecho.com

Ads run on Wednesdays; you must submit your ad by the previous Friday at 11 am. The costs are $18 for three lines, $6 for each additional line.

Irish Voice
432 Park Ave. S., Suite 1503, New York (212) 684-3366
www.irishvoice.com

Ads run on Wednesdays; you must submit your ad by the previous Monday at 4 pm. Thirty words cost $38.50 for one week or $72 for two weeks.

The nanny agencies listed below are ones we used or ones our friends recommended:

Larchmont Employment Agency
4 Gilder St. & Larchmont Ave., Larchmont (914) 834-1611
www.thelarchmontagency.com

Domestically Yours
535 Fifth Ave., New York (212) 986-1900

Frances Stuart Agency
1220 Lexington Ave., New York (212) 439-9222

To search for a nanny agency *(and also order a background check or use the nanny tax calculator)* try this website: **www.nannynetwork.com**.

Au Pairs

"Au pair," literally translated from French, means "on par"— as in, this person is not an employee but a temporary member of your family. These young *(generally eighteen- to twenty-six-year-old)* foreign women are usually in college or have just completed their studies. They come from all over the world to take part in a one-year "cultural exchange program" with a host family in the United States. They should be included in family meals, activities and outings or trips. In return for free room and board, they help out with your child care needs, but not with things like housework, cooking or laundry *(except as it relates to the kids)*.

By law, au pairs are not allowed to care for infants less than three months old. If they wish to be placed with a family who has a child under two, they must have completed 200 documented hours of child care, but they are still not child care professionals and may have limited experience. Nevertheless, they can form wonderful relationships with your children, and your children will have the opportunity to learn about other countries and cultures *(and maybe even a second language!)*. Au pairs are generally paid $140-250 per week.

145

Before you decide that this relatively inexpensive option is the one for you, here are a few important facts to consider.

There are significant up-front costs. Most au pair agencies get around $5,000 to cover visa costs, training and commissions. Also, you must pay up to $500 towards the au pair's post-secondary education, as she is required to take six class credits while in the U.S.

Hours are strictly regulated. You cannot have an au pair work more than ten hours a day and forty-five hours a week. They are required to have one full weekend off each month and a day-and-a-half off every week. However, unlike other caregivers, their schedules are generally far more flexible, which is ideal if your schedule fluctuates frequently.

Their duties are limited to child-related responsibilities. She is not required to do heavy housework or chores, like cooking for the entire family. However, some au pairs enjoy cooking, sewing or have other skills that they may want to share with their host families. Because au pairs must have international driver's licenses, they can also take care of bringing your child to school or to classes.

Congratulations, you just had a 19 year-old girl! Often families who take on au pairs feel like they've adopted a teenager. These girls are interested in the same things all girls their age are—shopping, socializing and, well, boys. You have not imported a nun, so make sure you have the nerves to deal with her social life.

An au pair can only stay with a family for twelve months. There will be some difficult good-byes. And the "changing of the guard," as the new au pair arrives, can be tough for your family and especially for your children.

To find an accredited au pair agency, contact the Department of State at **(202) 401-9810** or http://exchanges.state.gov/education/jexchanges/private/aupair.htm

Baby-sitters

Maybe you've been enjoying staying home with your newborn, but now you're ready to have a little "you time." Maybe you're just looking for someone to give you some freedom in your week—a few hours to shop, work out or grab lunch with a girlfriend. Or maybe you want to start "dating" your hubby again—whether it's a night out once in a while or every Saturday night. It's time to find a baby-sitter. And we guarantee you, you'll be glad you did. Just remember, the steadier the gig, the easier it is to line up a super sitter.

Of course, the best place to find a baby-sitter is through a referral from a friend or neighbor, but you'll find that even your closest friends may clam up when it comes to revealing the name of their precious Saturday Night Sitter. They may be willing, however, to see if their sitter has a friend who's available. Also check with high-school-age kids and senior citizens in your neighborhood. And keep your eyes and ears open. A friend of ours was grocery shopping and—desperate for an evening out with his wife—asked the clerk if she baby-sat. When she arrived later that night and his wife saw the multiple piercings and technicolor hair she was understandably panicked. But the sitter got along great with the kids, lived right down the street and had her own car. Now she baby-sits for them two afternoons and Saturday night every week. So you never know.

If you don't want to go out every Saturday night, you might want to hook up with a friend or neighbor to share a sitter; if you guarantee her a regular gig, it'll be a more stable arrangement for all of you. There are also services that provide sitters. Although they won't necessarily guarantee that the person you love will be yours every Saturday evening, they are a great source for experienced help. And in case your favorite sitter is in demand, you might want to line up several once-in-a-while sitters, so that you have group of sitters whom you are comfortable with to choose from. You should expect to pay a baby-sitter $8–12 an hour.

In addition to the clerks at the supermarket, you might want to try the following resources to find a baby-sitter.

Hartsdale Fire Station
300 W. Hartsdale Ave., Hartsdale (914) 949-2325

Sponsors an annual "Baby Sitters Course," consisting of twenty hours of specialized training in how to care for children and handle emergency situations. The fire station provides a list of course graduates as a public service.

Chappaqua Library
195 S. Greeley Ave., Chappaqua (914) 238-4779

This library course trains sitters ages ten and up. Visit the library to see the list of baby-sitting graduates.

The Service
(914) 834-7050

Serves lower Westchester only. Sitters get $9 an hour *(with a four-hour minimum)* plus a $4 transportation fee. An agency fee of $11 covers twenty hours of sitting.

Larchmont Employment Agency
4 Gilder St. & Larchmont Ave., Larchmont (914) 834-1611
www.thelarchmontagency.com

Sitters get $12–15 an hour, depending on experience level. The agency fee is 30% on top of that *(e.g., $3.60–$4.50 an hour)*.

There are also many less formal ways to find a sitter. Many local high schools, synagogues and churches have job boards and can be a great source for baby-sitters. In addition, you can post an ad on MonsterTRAK, a website for college students. You can target local campuses, including Manhattanville, Mercy, Sarah Lawrence and SUNY Purchase, and run your ad for two weeks for $25 per school. Contact this site at **(800) 999-8725** or **www.monstertrak.com**.

If you find sitters you like through one of these avenues, you'll want to make sure they are well prepared for the job —particularly if they're young. For a baby-sitting course that covers caring for and supervising children, preventing accidents and what to do in an emergency, contact the resources listed above or the Red Cross.

American Red Cross
Westchester County Chapter:
106 N. Broadway, White Plains (914) 946-6500
westchestercounty.redcross.org

Greenwich Chapter:
231 E. Putnam Ave., Greenwich, CT (203) 869-8444
www.greenwich.ctredcross.org

Baby-Sitter's Training is offered frequently. This eight-hour course is designed for adolescents eleven years and older and includes numerous hands-on learning experiences. Participants receive a Baby-Sitter's Guide, a checklist, and a Red Cross Certificate.

Savvy Suggestions

Avoid a last-minute rush before you go out by having on hand a pre-typed information list for your baby-sitter as well as a list of emergency numbers by every phone. Leave a "fill in the blank" line where you can write in the phone number of your destination.

Baby Nurses & Doulas

A baby nurse lives in for a week or two, but some families desire the extra help for far longer. She is there to assist you with new-baby care twenty-four hours a day. A baby nurse will bottle-feed the baby or bring the baby to you to breastfeed. She will assist with bathing, changing diapers, doing laundry and anything else you need to help get you settled with your newborn. Most importantly, she will help you get some rest, whether it's daytime naps or rocking the baby back to sleep after a middle-of-the-night feeding. Baby nurses generally cost $120–150 per day, and you provide room and board. While she will be available to you 24/7 during her stay, if you plan on keeping her longer than two weeks you will need to arrange for one or more days off.

Beyond getting a referral from a friend, there are also many agencies that place baby nurses; if you think you're interested in hiring one through an agency, be sure to register in advance. Generally, they can't guarantee you a specific person since, if you give birth early, she may already be working on another job. Although it runs contrary to every maternal instinct you have (*or will have*), you may end up hiring a baby nurse "sight unseen." When Betsy hired her baby nurse she was only able to speak with a mother who had used the same woman. Beyond that she had to trust that the agency she was dealing with was as good as everyone said it was. She was reassured by the agency's promise that if she wasn't comfortable with the nurse for any reason they would find a replacement right away. As it turned out, her nurse was wonderful and Betsy has recommended her highly to other moms. There are some baby nurses that work independently, in which case you may be able to meet them in advance and "reserve them" for your due date.

In addition to pregnancy and labor support, doula services provide postpartum support for moms and babies up to three months. Services can include infant care, sibling care, cooking meals, errands, light housekeeping and transportation to doctor's visits. There is usually a required minimum number of hours, and this care isn't cheap, averaging about $25 an hour. But if you don't have family nearby—or if you just want a professional to help you stay sane—doulas can certainly be a worthwhile investment *(and may be covered by your insurance)*. A doula comes to your house for a few hours at a time. Generally, you pay for a block of hours (*the minimum is usually twenty*), and you can use these any way you want to. To locate a doula, contact Doulas of North America at **(888) 788-DONA** or **www.dona.org**. Or contact one of the following local doula agencies:

Beyond Birth
393 Granite Springs Rd., Yorktown (914) 245-BABY

The Good Birth Company
114 Boutonville Rd., S. Salem (914) 763-5376

Background Checks & Nanny Cams

If you've picked a child care provider, but still want a little extra comfort, there are many services that can provide it. You may want to order a background check, particularly if your nanny didn't come through an agency *(which will usually do it for you)*. In addition, if you're so inclined, you can buy or rent a "nanny cam," which will allow you to videotape activities in your home. Another option is remote video monitoring, which allows you to keep an eye on your home from anywhere at any time, via a high-speed, always-on internet connection like DSL or cable modem. One suggestion: if you hire more than one nanny in your child's life, or plan on monitoring for an extended period of time, in many cases you can buy a system for the same cost as renting it.

Care Check
1056 Fifth Ave., New York (212) 360-6640

Offers video surveillance sales *(approximately $999)* and remote video monitoring *(approximately $2100)*. Rentals are also available *($250 for two days or $350 for three days)*, and you can apply the cost of the rental to a future sale.

Icam1

www.icam1.com (914) 741-1991

Offers remote video monitoring *($2300–2600, and ongoing service is $1 per day)*. Provides free in-home estimates.

Knowyournanny.com

300 Grand River Blvd., Dover Township, NJ (888) MYBABY-1
www.knowyournanny.com

Provides background checks, including a state criminal check, a driver's license check and a credit check *($129)*. Offers video surveillance sales *($199–369)* as well as rentals *($99.95 for ten days)*. Also offers remote video monitoring *(approximately $800)*.

Nanny Check

6-05 Saddle River Rd. #111, Fair Lawn, NJ (800) 788-3937
www.nannycheck.com

Provides a variety of packages for pre-employment screening and background checks, including criminal, civil and sexual offender records *($49–300+)*. Also offers video surveillance sales *($300–700)* and rentals *(approximately $100 per week)*.

Employment Tax Services

The first year Laura had a nanny, she was dismayed to learn that the accountant who had been doing the family taxes didn't know how to fill out the Schedule H for household employers. So she found an accountant who could educate her about this federal tax form, as well as W2s and W3s, state tax requirements, unemployment insurance, workers compensation, disability insurance and more. If you have the time and inclination, you can certainly file these forms on your own.

Those of you who don't like filling out tax forms each quarter may want to find some help. See the following resources:

GTM Associates
7 Halfmoon Executive Pk. Dr., Clifton Park, NY
(888) 4EASYPAY/(518) 373-4111
www.gtmassociates.com

Household tax and payroll services.

Household Employment Taxes Online
www.householdemploymenttaxes.com

An on-line service for household payroll and taxes, plus free resources for do-it-yourselfers.

Nannytax
50 E. 42nd St., Suite 2108, New York
(888) NANNYTAX/(212) 867-1776
www.nannytax.com

Full-service tax preparation for employers of domestic help.

You Gotta Have Friends

Support Groups
Newcomers Clubs

When you first get home with that bundle of joy, it can be a very daunting experience. Particularly if it's your first. Because this can also be a very isolating time, the best thing you can do is reach out to other moms.

Take Laura's experience, for instance. Having mastered lots of other challenges at work and at home, Laura found herself on maternity leave and at her wit's end—with just a touch of the "baby blues." So she figured that she would approach mommy networking just like professional networking. When Sam was born she put the word out to everyone she knew that she was looking for other new moms to connect with. Sometimes moms responded the way you might to a pushy telemarketer. But sometimes it worked. Through the "six degrees of separation" rule *(via the aunt of one of Laura's college friends)*, she was introduced to a mom with a son born just a week after Sam. *(And he was also named Sam!)* They clicked right away and became fast friends. The thing is, when it comes to dealing with all those intense emotions, nothing beats a girlfriend who understands exactly what you're going through. So don't be shy. You never know who you'll meet.

It's no surprise that one of the other things Laura threw herself into while on maternity leave was helping to found the local chapter of Mothers & More, a social and support group for moms. In the three short years it's been around, membership has quadrupled, making it one of the most popular organizations for Westchester moms to join. It's also how Betsy (who led the group for several years) and Laura became friends—and the rest, as they say, is history.

Many hospitals also sponsor support groups, including general support and discussion groups for new moms. Some classes focus on a specific topic, such as breastfeeding, child safety, CPR, baby care or adapting to parenthood, and some address a specific group, such as mothers of multiples. You can participate even if you didn't deliver your child at that hospital, so call for information *(see our listings in Chapter 15)*. Also check with your community centers *(see our listings in Chapter 3)*, as they run many such programs. For more information, check out **www.newcomersclub.com** and **www.westchestergov.com** *(under family services),* or call the Westchester Self-Help Clearinghouse, which maintains a comprehensive database of parenting support groups, at (914) 949-7699.

Support Groups

ADOPTIVE PARENTS COMMITTEE
(914) 997-7859
hudsonapc@yahoo.com
www.adoptiveparents.org

CHAPPAQUA PRESCHOOL PARENTING ASSOCIATION
(914) 238-0809

155

KATONAH VILLAGE LIBRARY NEW MOTHERS' GROUP
(914) 232-3508

LATINA MOTHERS' NETWORK
Northern Westchester Hospital
(914) 666-1111
www.nwhc.net

MOM'S CLUB OF RYE BROOK
(914) 937-6626

MOTHERS & MORE
Lower Westchester chapter: (914) 722-1008
www.mothersandmore.org

THE MOTHER'S CONNECTION
(914) 737-8976

MOTHERS OF MULTIPLES
Larchmont chapter: Sophie Dassesse-Cowles (914) 833-5011
Westchester/Putnam chapter: 914-273-3913
twinmom9997@aol.com
(both are affiliated with the National Organization of Mothers of Twins Clubs)
www.nomotc.org

MOPS *(Mothers of Preschoolers)*
Bedford Hills
(914) 666-5384

NEW MOMS SUPPORT GROUP
(914) 666-1370

NEW MOMMIES' NETWORK
(212) 665-7956
www.newmommies.com

NEW MOTHERS TALKING
Hudson Valley Hospital Center
(914) 736-0218
www.hvhc.org/wellness.html

PARENTS WITHOUT PARTNERS
(914) 260-0592
www.pwpchapter21.com

THE PLACE FOR SINGLE PARENTS
Jewish Community Center of Mid-Westchester
(914) 472-3300, ext. 412
www.mwjcc.org

ROCKLAND PARENT-CHILD CENTER
(845) 358-2702

SINGLE PARENT SUPPORT GROUP
White Plains chapter: (914) 761-3584
Nyack chapter: (845) 358-2702

TWINS PLUS CLUB
(914) 736-9633

Newcomers Clubs

CHAPPAQUA PARENTS PRESCHOOL ASSOCIATION
(For residents of the New Castle community)
(914) 320-CPPA
hlwny@hotmail.com

LARCHMONT NEWCOMERS CLUB
(For residents of Larchmont, Mamaroneck and New Rochelle)
(914) 973-LNC1

PLEASANTVILLE PARENTS PRESCHOOL ASSOCIATION
rapley@mindspring.com

NEWCOMERS CLUB OF POUND RIDGE
(914) 764-5172
cshepre@aol.com

Savvy Suggestion

Great Places to Meet Other New Moms

* The women's room at Nordstrom or Neiman Marcus at The Westchester. (Also great for breastfeeding.)
* A Mommy & Me program, or other classes for newborns.
* Your neighborhood—get outside with that carriage and take a walk!
* Your local playground. Even if their children are too small to play, mothers congregate there anyway.
* Starbucks—if you get an empathic smile, start a conversation!
* Any store that carries baby stuff is a great place to compare notes and share sleep deprivation stories.

PURCHASE NEWCOMERS CLUB

(For residents of Purchase, West Harrison and Harrison)
newcomers1@hotmail.com

RYE NEWCOMERS CLUB

(For residents of Rye, Rye Brook and Port Chester)
ryenewcomers@yahoo.com

SCARSDALE/HARTSDALE NEWCOMERS CLUB

(For residents of Scarsdale, Hartsdale and Edgemont)
vgfam@aol.com

SOMERS NEWCOMERS CLUB

(For residents of Somers)
sncpresident@yahoo.com

Where do I...?

Where Do I Get My Child's Hair Cut?
How Do I Childproof My House?
How Do I Fake a Home-Cooked Meal?
Where Can I Fill a Prescription for Croup Medicine at 3 am?
Where Can I Get My Child's Portrait Taken?

There are tons of books out there that answer the simple questions, such as "How do I wean my baby?" So we thought we'd attack the truly *complicated* issues of parenthood, like where to take your child for his first haircut or where to find "take out" food that's as good as homemade. Seriously, we know what it's like to need some good suggestions about "the little things." Hopefully these listings of helpful services will make your life a little easier.

159

"Where Do I Get My Child's Hair Cut?"

Some kids sprout a full head of hair very early on, while some resemble Phil Collins longer than we might like; either way, when the time finally comes for that first haircut (*and the many thereafter*), there seem to be more and more places popping up in Westchester where you can go to get it done. Sam needed a haircut by the time he was three months old, and about every two months since. The novelty vehicle seats, TV monitors and full range of popular videos that seem to work so well for the other kids don't seem to distract him a bit from the task at hand; hopefully, you'll have better luck with your child.

If it's your child's first haircut, most places offer to preserve a lock of hair and give you a certificate commemorating this momentous event. Generally all of these places will take you on a walk-in basis, but we recommend making an appointment to keep waiting time to a minimum.

BEDFORD HILLS
Kidstyles
701 N. Bedford Rd. (914) 666-7707
Hours: Monday 9:30 am–6 pm, Tuesday–Friday 9:30am–5:30 pm, Saturday 9 am–3 pm

CHAPPAQUA
Cool Kidz Kutz
18 S. Greely Ave. (914) 238-2817
Hours: Monday–Wednesday 9:30 am–5 pm, Thursday–Friday 9 am–6:30 pm, Saturday 9 am–4:30 pm

LARCHMONT
Fun Cuts
2100 Boston Post Rd. (914) 834-5300
Hours: Monday, Wednesday, Friday and Saturday 9 am–5 pm, Thursday 9 am–6:30 pm, Sunday 10 am–3 pm

SCARSDALE
Cool Kuts for Kids
450 Central Ave. (914) 472-6400
Hours: Tuesday–Saturday 10 am–5 pm

Happy Kids Haircuts
832 Scarsdale Ave. (914) 725-2044
Hours: Monday-Friday 10 am–6 pm, Saturday 11 am-5 pm, Sunday 11 am-4pm

RIVERDALE
Someplace Special for Kids
492 West 238th St., Bronx (718) 432-6622
www.someplacespecialforkids.com
Hours: Tuesday–Saturday 10 am–6 pm, Sunday 11 am–5 pm

CONNECTICUT
Lesli's Barber Shop
1 Hyde St. (*off of Hope St.*), Stamford (203) 329-8315
Hours: Wednesday–Saturday 8:30 am–5 pm

Subway Barber Shop
315 Greenwich Ave., Greenwich (203) 869-3263
Hours: Daily 8 am–5 pm, closed Wednesdays and Sundays

PUTNAM COUNTY
Short Cuts
441 Rte. 6, Mahopac (845) 621-2969
Hours: Tuesday–Friday 9:30 am–5:30 pm, Thursdays 9:30 am–
7 pm, Saturday 9 am–5 pm

"How Do I Childproof My House?"

The first step in childproofing your house is to know your child. Some kids will open every cabinet and be inexplicably drawn to the most dangerous items therein, while some will happily ignore them. Simon, for example, was never very interested in opening cabinets, and to the extent that he tried he was deterred with a simple rubber band wrapped around the knobs *(By the way, we're told this is a bad idea, since rubber bands can break and become a choking hazard).* The truth of the matter is, you can buy every childproofing product on the market, and it won't guarantee that your child will never get hurt. Most children we know can unlock a childproof lock quicker than their parents can. But, better safe than sorry, right?

> ### Savvy Suggestion
>
> Leave one kid-level drawer or cabinet un-child-proofed and fill it with unbreakables that are safe for your child to play with *(e.g., Tupperware, wooden spoons).* If your child gets frustrated by the other locked doors, you can point him to "his drawer" and let the games begin.

As your child becomes more mobile, for the minimum in safety, you'll probably want to plug up outlets, cushion sharp corners and move the Drano to a high shelf. Then, once you've determined your needs, visit one of the larger

161

baby stores listed in Chapter 11. They carry a wide range of do-it-yourself equipment—from baby gates to toilet seat locks—and the staff can generally answer your questions and point you in the right direction. If you would feel more comfortable having professional input, we've listed below a few services you may want to check into.

CHILD PROOFERS
(800) 642-4654/(914) 381-5106
www.childproofersinc.com

For over twelve years, Child Proofers has been doing in-home evaluations and installations and designing customized childproofing solutions. They are members of the International Association for Child Safety *(www.iafcs.org)* and carry some products that are exclusive to the professional childproofing industry.
Cost: An in-home evaluation is free; installation is $75 per hour, plus the cost of the products.

KIDS SAFE CHILDPROOFING
(877) 842-KIDS/(203) 925-8622
www.ekidssafe.com

Trained by a certified teaching facility, these childproofers will help you identify your needs as well as install the products you purchase, including safety gates, cabinet and drawer latches, plastic for railings, appliance latches, fire safety products and more.
Cost: An in-home evaluation is $25, which can be credited towards a future purchase.

Savvy Suggestion

Need help making sure your car seat is correctly and safely installed? Many local police and fire departments hold car seat inspection weeks, but they'll usually check yours anytime. Call for details.

"How Do I Fake a Home-Cooked Meal?"

There are lots of ways to have a healthy, wholesome meal at home without cooking. Supermarkets and gourmet stores offer a wide variety of prepared foods to choose from, such as rotisserie chicken, pastas, fish, side dishes and more.

BOSTON MARKET
Westchester Locations:
667 W. Boston Post Rd., Mamaroneck (914) 777-1017
130 N. Bedford Rd., Mount Kisco (914) 241-8800
77 Quaker Ridge Rd., New Rochelle (914) 235-0550
650 Central Park Ave., Scarsdale (914) 472-5038
32 Xavier Dr., Yonkers (914) 963-1305
Connecticut Locations:
1345 E. Putnam Ave., Old Greenwich (203) 637-4088
1018 High Ridge Rd., Stamford (203) 321-1410

Boston Market sells an entire meal that includes your choice of a whole chicken, a pound of turkey or ham, or an entire meatloaf, plus three large side dishes and cornbread, for under $17.

163

Savvy Suggestion

Hit the salad bar at your local supermarket for fresh, pre-chopped ingredients that take less than a minute to assemble. Pour your favorite dressing into the plastic container at home and shake it to create a perfectly tossed, garden-fresh salad.

You can use the same trick for a sensational stir-fry shortcut. Get some multi-colored peppers, carrots, mushrooms, onions and baby corn, throw them in a pan with some seasonings and voila! Now you're cookin', baby!

Another convenient alternative is this service we've discovered, which delivers for a wide range of restaurants.

WAITER ON THE RUN
(800) 460-0090
www.waterontherun.com

Help is just a phone call away. They will place and deliver your food order from one of over a dozen local restaurants, including California Pizza Kitchen *(pizza and pasta)*, Casa Maya & Taqueria Mariachi Loco *(Mexican)*, Epstein Brothers *(deli)*, Sakura *(Japanese)*, Central Square Café *(American)* and more. You can place your order in advance and request a specific delivery time so that dinner is ready when you are. Currently they service only central and lower Westchester.
Hours: 11:30 am–10 pm
Cost: $4.99 delivery fee plus 15% tip (credit cards accepted); $20 lunch minimum, $15 dinner minimum *(food total, not including fee and tip)*.

"Where Can I Fill a Prescription for Croup Medicine at 3 am?"

Things like croup and vomiting seem to only occur in the wee hours of the night, making them extra challenging to deal with. However, there are two pharmacies in Westchester that are open twenty-four hours a day. So while you're sitting in the steam-filled bathroom singing to your baby, your spouse can head to one of the following pharmacies.

CVS LARCHMONT
1310 Boston Post Rd.
Front Store Phone: (914) 833-3307
Pharmacy Phone: (914) 833-3001

CVS WHITE PLAINS
452 Mamaroneck Ave.
Front Store Phone: (914) 686-0228
Pharmacy Phone: (914) 686-0226

"Where Can I Get My Child's Portrait Taken?"

In addition to the many professional photographers in the area, a less expensive alternative is to go to one of the major photo centers around Westchester. All the studios listed below offer cost-saving packages. They have a variety of cute backdrops and props, and you can just walk in to most of them without setting up an appointment. Check their websites for coupons and special offers.

JC PENNEY PORTRAIT STUDIO
www.jcpenneyportraits.com
100 Main St., White Plains (718) 862-0051

SEARS PORTRAIT STUDIO
www.searsportrait.com
275 Main St., White Plains (914) 997-5380
86 Cross County Center, Yonkers (914) 377-2169

THE PICTURE PEOPLE
www.picturepeople.com
100 Main St., White Plains (914) 428-2811
3661 Palisades Center Dr., West Nyack (845) 353-6989

165

Savvy Savings

Find the cheapest price for gas by logging onto **www.westchestergov.com**. There is an area price comparison to locate the station with the lowest prices near you.

Attention All Shoppers!

Malls
Outlet Centers
Toy Stores
Baby Stuff
Kids' Furniture
Online Grocery Shopping
Personalized Baby & Toddler Gifts
Bicycles

Westchester is a shopper's paradise. There are several fantastic malls, loads of specialty shops and even a couple of outlet centers nearby for the bargain hunter in all of us. While the choices may seem limitless out there, we're going to share a few of our favorites.

Malls

GALLERIA MALL AT WHITE PLAINS
100 Main St., White Plains (914) 682-0111
www.galleriaatwhiteplains.com

Hours: Monday-Saturday 10 am-9:30 pm, Sunday 11 am-7 pm
Stores Include: Bunnies (914) 328-3130, The Children's Place (914) 997-8133, The Disney Store (914) 684-0320, GapKids (914) 997-8118, H&M (914) 422-3777, K*B Toys (914) 948-6686, Kids Foot Locker (914) 421-1857, Old Navy (914) 682-0482, The Picture People (914) 428-2811
What to Know Before You Go: You can rent strollers shaped like cars and trucks at the customer service booth on

the food court level *($5 for a single stroller, $6 for a double)*. Only one of the strollers comes equipped with an infant seat.

JEFFERSON VALLEY MALL

650 Lee Blvd., Yorktown Heights (914) 245-4200
www.shopsimon.com

Hours: Monday-Saturday 10 am-9:30 pm, Sunday 11 am-6 pm
Stores Include: BabyGap (914) 245-9013, The Children's Place, (914) 245-8818, dELIA*s (914) 962-4266, The Disney Store (914) 245-7345, GapKids (914) 245-9013, Gymboree (914) 243-0625, H&M (914) 962-6660, K*B Toys (914) 245-8274, The Limited Too (914) 962-5119, Macy's (914) 962-9100, The Picture People (914) 245-3151, Sears (914) 248-2500, Stride Rite (914) 245-8553
What to Know Before You Go: There is also a large food court and an eight-screen United Artists Theater.

PALISADES CENTER

1000 Palisades Center Dr., West Nyack (845) 348-1000
www.palisadescenter.com

Exit 12 off the New York State Thruway (87) will deposit you at the second largest indoor mall in America. This amazing combination of shopping, entertainment and recreation facilities boasts over 250 specialty shops, twelve restaurants, the unique ThEATery area, an NHL-size ice-skating rink, a sixty-eight-foot Ferris wheel, a restored antique carousel, a twenty-one-screen Loews Theatre and a state-of-the-art IMAX Theatre.
Hours: Monday-Saturday 10 am-9:30 pm, Sunday 11 am-7 pm
The movie theater and restaurants remain open later.
Stores Include: Filene's (845) 358-7990, JC Penney (845) 348-0382, Lord & Taylor (845) 358-4672, Barnes & Noble (845) 348-4701, Bed, Bath & Beyond (845) 348-9371, BJ's Wholesale Club (845) 353-9312, Home Depot (845) 348-0566, and Target (845) 348-6440. **Kids' stores include:** abercrombie (845) 348-7044, BabyGap (845) 358-8381, Build A Bear Workshop (845) 353-1895, Gymboree (845) 358-5336, H&M (845) 727-1958, K*B Toys (845) 353-2232, Kids Footlocker, Limited Too (845) 353-4628, Old Navy (845) 348-0993,

Payless Shoe Source (845) 348-4761, Picture People (845) 353-6989, Stride Rite (845) 727-5062, The Disney Store (845) 348-9262

What to Know Before You Go: Novelty vehicles on each floor will give your child a short ride for a couple of quarters. There is also a ride-on train outside JC Penney on Level 1 of the mall. The ride costs $2, but it lasts long enough that you'll feel you're getting your money's worth. Although the center is vast, it still can get pretty packed on the weekends during prime shopping hours. Go early to avoid lines at the kid's attractions. And once you think you've done it all, don't forget to take your kids on a ride in the glass elevators. Lastly, when we say this place is huge, we mean it's massive—so don't even think of going without a stroller. They are available to rent if you forget yours.

THE WESTCHESTER
125 Westchester Ave., White Plains (914) 683-8600
www.shopsimon.com

This is the mall of all malls. Anchored by Nordstrom and Neiman Marcus, it contains more than 150 upscale stores. You know you're someplace special when you see the skylights above and the marble and carpeted floors below. The mall is laid out as three different "avenues," with a fountain and sculpture at the end of each.

Hours: Monday-Saturday 10 am-9 pm, Sunday 11 am-6 pm
Stores Include: abercrombie (914) 397-2268, BabyGap (914) 626-2319, The Children's Place (914) 997-1264, The Disney Store (914) 397-0528, FAO Schwarz (914) 946-4567, The Gamekeeper (914) 644-8622, GapKids (914) 644-8629, Gymboree (914) 644-8410, Hanna Andersson (914) 684-2410, Jacadi (914) 682-1600, Janie and Jack (914) 683-1924, K*B Toys (914) 761-0316, The Limited Too (914) 644-8762, Oilily (914) 328-8900, Stride Rite (914) 686-3584, Talbots Kids (914) 644-8280

What to Know Before You Go: Ample indoor parking is available, but for added convenience there is valet parking for an additional $2 charge. Strollers are available at both valet stands on Retail Level 2. The food court has all the usual fast food suspects, but you'll find a bevy of strollers parked outside of City Limits Diner, which is as kid-friendly as they come. Lines to get in can be long, so our advice is to go early or late or, better yet, make your husband wait in line while you and your child shop! A widely known "secret" is that the "ladies lounges" in Nordstrom and Neiman Marcus are the most pleasant place you'll find to breastfeed your baby. All mall bathrooms offer changing tables, and those labeled "family bathrooms" offer a tot-sized potty for children learning to use them.

Outlet Centers

If you're anything like Betsy, you approach shopping as you would a competitive sport. Outlet centers represent the ultimate score. You can find name-brand clothing, shoes and toys, usually at prices 20-70% less than you'd pay for them in the retail stores. Sure, the clothes they have in stock when you're there may not fit your child today, but just buy one size larger and wait. The best part is, with the money you save buying your kids' shoes at half price, you can justify picking up those designer shoes for yourself!

MANUFACTURER'S OUTLET CENTER
195 North Bedford Rd., Mount Kisco (914) 241-8503
http://www.westchesterweb.com/outlet/index.html

You'll find a Carter's Outlet (914) 241-7520 as well as Playscape (*an indoor play space which is described in Chapter 2*) and a couple of casual, family-friendly restaurants. There is also an A&P if you need to grab any necessities before heading home.
Hours: Monday-Saturday 10 am-9 pm, Sunday 12 pm-6 pm

WOODBURY COMMONS PREMIUM OUTLETS
498 Red Apple Court, Central Valley (845) 928-4000
www.premiumoutlets.com

This massive outlet center is located less than an hour north of central Westchester. It's worth the trip for the mind-boggling selection of premium stores with merchandise that is often still in season. We recommend stocking up on clothing mainstays in several different sizes so that you're all set as your child grows.

Hours: Monday-Saturday 10 am-9 pm, Sunday 10 am-8 pm

Stores Include: Carter's Childrenswear (845) 928-9498, The Children's Place Outlet (845) 928-5365, Gap Outlet (845) 928-3122, JM Originals (845) 928-5125, K*B Toy Outlet (845) 928-9424, Little Me (845) 928-7343, Oilily (845) 928-4384, OshKosh B'Gosh (845) 928-4449, Petit Bateau (845) 928-8850, Stride Rite Keds Sperry (845) 928-5104, World of Fun (845) 928-6012

What to Know Before You Go: This has been called the third biggest tourist site in New York, so you can imagine the crowds as the day goes on. Aim to get there early and try to park in the parking lot closest to the stores you want to check out. The website will show you all the store locations. But here's the real insider's secret—if you are a member of AAA, go to a customer service desk and pick up a free coupon book filled with additional savings. It can save you literally hundreds of dollars!

Savvy Style

Your kid can look like a million bucks without your spending a fortune on clothes. Be sure to check out chains like Marshall's and TJ Maxx for brand name clothes at a big discount, as well as stores like Target, Old Navy and H&M.

Toy Stores

Besides the traditional chains there are a few stand-out toy stores in the area. These smaller shops focus on customer service and boast an impressive knowledge of all their merchandise.

MILLERS
335 Mamaroneck Ave., Mamaroneck (914) 698-5070
www.millertoy.com

Millers has been around over for over fifty years *(it originally opened in Harlem)* and houses a remarkable selection of train hobby paraphernalia, bikes, outdoor swing sets, books, furniture and, of course, toys. They carry all the usual brands as well as a few harder-to-find ones. Many of the staff have worked there for years and are incredibly helpful. If they don't have something that you want, they'll get it for you. They even offer free gift wrapping and assembly services.
Hours: Monday-Saturday 9 am-6 pm, Thursday 9 am-7 pm

TRY & BUY
52 Pondfield Rd., Bronxville (914) 337-0074
196 Katonah Ave, Katonah (914) 232-1990
45 Washington Ave, Pleasantville (914) 769-2997

These small, well-stocked stores carry products that you might not find anywhere else. The staff are knowledgeable and if you go in not knowing exactly what you want to get for the slew of birthday parties your child has been invited to, they'll be able to help you find the perfect gift at the perfect price.
Hours: Monday-Saturday 9 am-6 pm *(Thursday until 7 pm)*, Sunday 12 pm-5 pm

LEARNING EXPRESS
21 Spencer Pl., Scarsdale (914) 723-3700
www.scarsdale.learningexpress.com

They have a good selection of toys, games, arts and crafts supplies, science kits, dolls and many other play items. They are geared towards carrying toys you might not find in

other places. They have a serious commitment to customer service and offer free gift wrapping, free personalization and "express lane service": if you call ahead they will select, wrap and personalize your gift and deliver it to you curbside so you never have to leave your car. *(A great thing if you've ever tried to find parking in Scarsdale village!)*
Hours: Monday-Saturday 9:30 am-6 pm, Sunday 11 am-4 pm

Baby Stuff

When it comes to giving you the most choices, certainly bigger is better. There are two baby mega-stores every Westchester parent should know about.

BABIES "R" US

2700 Central Park Ave., Yonkers (914) 722-4500
www.babiesrus.com

The newer of the two baby emporiums, this spacious, multilevel store has it all. Part of the Toys "R" Us/Kids "R" Us family, this store caters to children ages 0-2, with baby gear, clothing, furniture, toys, supplies, strollers, bedding, books and more. At times, finding sales help can be challenging, and they're not as familiar with all the products as we'd have liked. However, they do have the largest selection of merchandise and it's a great place to go if you know exactly what you"re looking for.
Hours: Monday-Saturday 9:30 am-9:30 pm, Sunday 11 am-7 pm

Savvy Suggestion

Do your shopping and delight your child at the same time. Some area supermarkets, like Food Emporium in Scarsdale and Stop & Shop in North White Plains, have shopping carts with toy cars attached to the front. They safely keep your child strapped in, and he'll love steering his way up and down the aisles.

BUY BUY BABY

1019 Central Park Ave, Scarsdale (914) 725-9220
www.buybuybaby.com

This store has everything for children ages 0-4. Again, you will find a staggering array of baby gear, clothing, furniture, toys, supplies, strollers, bedding, books and more. They have a staff that is readily available to help you and is generally very knowledgeable about products. They have a very convenient self-scanning system which makes registering a breeze. The aisles could be wider and we wished they had more places to stop and rest, but this is a great place to go when you only want to make one stop.

Hours: Monday-Saturday 9:30 am-9:30 pm, Sunday 11 am-6 pm

Kids' Furniture

While the baby megastores can't be beat when it comes to selection, Westchester has a lot of specialty shops and boutiques that you may also want to check out.

Here are some of our favorites for children's furniture:

BELLINI BABY AND TEEN DESIGNER FURNITURE

495 Central Park Ave., Scarsdale (914) 472-7336

This is a company that believes in quality over quantity. Every crib converts to a junior bed and they are the only store we know of that features a tall changing table that can transform into drawers with bookshelves, for when your child is out of diapers. The store features many hand-painted, personalized options for accenting your child's room and they also carry a few lines of bedding, including their exclusive styles. They have an in-home delivery and assembly service starting at $85.

Hours: Monday-Saturday 10 am-6 pm (*Thursday until 7 pm*), Sunday 12 pm-5 pm

MILLERS

335 Mamaroneck Ave., Mamaroneck (914) 698-5070
www.millertoy.com

In addition to toys, Millers also has a small but sweet
selection of baby furniture. Though only a few cribs and
pieces of furniture are on display, you can look through
catalogs to find the perfect items to order for your nursery.
They specialize in several European brands but can get you
the most popular American ones as well. The staff is helpful
and experienced, and if you have another child in tow, she
or he will most likely be mesmerized by the train display,
giving you a chance to get your shopping done.
Hours: Monday-Saturday 9 am-6 pm, Thursday 9 am-7 pm

CRIB & TEEN CITY EXPO

183 South Central Park Ave., Hartsdale (914) 686-3331
159 Rte. 4 West, Paramus, NJ (201) 843-1505
www.cribteencity.com

A recent addition to the area, this store strikes a comfortable balance between the high-end boutiques and the baby
megastores. Their slogan is, "We take your baby from cradle
to college," so it's no surprise that you'll find a wide range
of furniture to select from. And for the "big kids," they have
a superb assortment of twin beds, bunk beds, loft/desk
combinations and more. One especially nice feature is a
complimentary in-home consulting service to help you
make just the right choices. They also carry bedding to
complete the look.
Hours: Monday, Wednesday and Thursday 10 am-9 pm,
Tuesday, Friday and Saturday 10 am-6 pm, Sunday 11 am-5 pm

WENDY GEE HOME ACCESSORIES

29 King St., Chappaqua (914) 238-1241
1949 Palmer Ave., Larchmont (914) 834-8507

If you're looking for something unique and whimsical, this
is the place. Although they carry tons of adorable gifts and
accessories, they also are one of the largest retailers of
"Maine Cottage" furniture, which they sell at a 15% discount.

Maine Cottage is known for their high-quality pieces, offered in a kaleidoscope of colors, which may still be around *(and in style)* even after the kids are off to college. The bigger of the two stores is in Larchmont, but both stores have a good selection of samples on the floor. You can also check out all the furniture choices at www.maincottage.com.
Hours: Monday-Saturday 9:30 am-6 pm

If you are looking for something a little more personal, there are several stores that specialize in custom-made furniture. They will build a bed, desk, bookshelf or even bunk bed to suit your style and needs exactly. When ordering custom furniture you have to expect about a ten-to-twelve-week turnaround time, so it's not the way to go if you need something quickly. However, if you can be patient the results can be well worth the wait.

KID'S SUPPLY CO.

14 Railroad Ave., Greenwich, CT (203) 422-2100
www.kidssupplyco.com

If you're looking for both style and substance, this is a store you won't want to miss. They do have quite a few items in stock, but the real specialty of this store is custom-made furniture for children; the items have been featured in many children's and design magazines. They do not make cribs but do carry several ready-made lines. They create custom bedding as well. They also have a store in Manhattan, call for hours.
Hours: Monday-Friday 9:30 am-5:30 pm, Saturday 10 am-5 pm

GO TO YOUR ROOM

234 Mill St., Greenwich, CT (203) 532-9701
www.gotoyourroom.com

Fernando Martinez and his wife have been running this store for years. Fernando is a master craftsman and designer, and they also have an artist on staff who can custom-paint anything, from headboards to drawer pulls, to complete the look of your child's room. Though they do not carry any cribs, they do have custom-made bedding and other items to accent your child's room.

Hours: Monday-Saturday 10:30 am-5 pm

Online Grocery Shopping

It's a scene you know all too well—it's raining and you've managed to wrangle your child out of the car and into a shopping cart. You're halfway through your grocery list when you reach the dreaded cereal aisle. The battle ensues. You just wanted to pick up some healthy, low-fat flakes for yourself and your daughter is screaming for the bright box with her favorite cartoon character on it *(only 39 grams of sugar per serving)*.

Thank goodness for the internet. Now you can get your grocery shopping done whenever it's convenient for you, and you can even stock up on necessities like jumbo quantities of diapers, wipes, baby formula and more. Some delivery fees apply, and some of these sites don't necessarily offer as wide a selection as going to a store. But they do deliver —and not just right to your door, but into your house! This is a major benefit for anyone who has ever dragged both a twenty-pound toddler and a twenty-pound container of laundry detergent up a flight of stairs.

www.peapod.com
Offered through Stop & Shop Supermarkets, this service has a website that is very easy to use. You can use your Stop & Shop card number to take advantage of extra discounts, and when you select a particular item, if a comparable item is on sale they will let you know. You can even redeem coupons when the driver arrives with your groceries. Once you've purchased through the site, you can store your "shopping cart" of frequently bought items to speed up future visits. If you place your order prior to 11 am you can often get delivery that same day, otherwise next-day delivery is available and you select a time that is convenient for you. **Cost:** Minimum order is $50. Delivery fees are $4.95 for orders over $75 and $9.95 for orders less than $75.

www.yourgrocer.com

This warehouse club carries the major brands you'll find at a Costco or Sam's Club, but there is no membership fee. You can stock up on heavy items like cases of soda, laundry detergent and cleaning supplies; they also carry fresh produce, meat and baked goods. You can store your shopping list on their site, to speed up your future virtual visits, and next-day delivery is almost always available.

Cost: Minimum order is $75 *(excluding tax and delivery)*. Delivery fee is $9.95.

Personalized Baby & Toddler Gifts

These are great presents: they're personal, thoughtful and impossible to re-gift. There's practically no end to what you can paint or embroider a child's name on. From burp cloths and blankets to rocking chairs and step stools, it's a great way to welcome a new baby into the house or to make a new big brother or big sister feel special. There are a lot of stores in Westchester that will personalize gift items, but here are a few standouts.

LOIS REITER LTD.

15 Rye Ridge Plaza (*at Bowman Ave.*), Rye Brook
(914) 937-7685

The store is packed with great gifts for newborns, young children and adults. Lois and her knowledgeable staff will help you find the perfect gift, even if it's for the child who has everything. Bibs, burp clothes, clothing, blankets, stools, table and chair sets, even personalized hangers—if you can fit a child's name on it, chances are they carry it.

THIGAMAJIGS! BY ANDREA

(914) 762-8650
thigamajgs@aol.com

Uniquely personalized gifts for all ages and occasions. Andrea hand-paints a wide variety of wood and ceramic items, including picture frames, step stools, rocking chairs and toy chests, and she will work with you to create a theme *(trucks, moon and stars, hearts, etc.)* and choose the colors. Prices range from $6 to $300. She's located in central Westchester but will ship anywhere.

And for you internet junkies:

www.inastitch.com
Handmade embroidered items ranging from the expected to the unusual. They have a complete line of "quillows" *(a quilt that folds into a pillow)* that can be personalized for a truly one-of-a-kind gift.

www.mybambino.com
A remarkably extensive collection of personalized items, including baby gifts and furniture, toys and sports gifts, piggy banks, school supplies, even Madame Alexander dolls. You can even get your child a personalized book for potty training *(as Betsy did for Simon)* that mentions where he lives and refers to his best friend by name.

www.personalizedforbaby.com
This site also specializes in embroidered gifts but includes hand-painted items as well. They will do gift baskets to fit any budget, and if you're not sure about a friend's taste they even have gift certificates.

Bicycles

What's nicer on a warm day than rallying the troops for a family bike trip? Check out Chapter 1 to find a park with a bike path near you. You can equip your bike with a trailer or bike seat so that even the youngest child can tag along and, as he gets older, you can buy him some wheels of his own. Here are some great places to get set up when you're ready to hit the road.

DANNY'S CYCLES
644 Central Park Ave., Scarsdale (914) 723-3408
www.dannyscycles.com

Danny, a second-generation bike dealer, definitely knows his stuff, and he and his staff provide friendly, personalized attention. Whether you're purchasing your child's first tricycle or outfitting the whole family for summertime outings, this is a great place to go. If your child is too young for her own set of wheels Danny and his knowledgeable staff can set you up with bike seats, trailers and other add-ons you can use to take your little one out for a spin. They also carry a wide range of safety equipment, including children's helmets.
Hours: Mondays 10 am-6 pm, Tuesday-Friday 10 am-9 pm, Saturday and Sunday 10 am-6 pm

MILLERS
335 Mamaroneck Ave., Mamaroneck (914) 698-5070
www.millertoy.com

See the listing under Toy Stores for more information.

PIERMONT BICYCLE CONNECTION
215 Ash St., Piermont (845) 365-0900
www.piermontbike.com

Piermont has always been a haven for cyclists because it's situated directly along 9W—a bike route stretching as far north as Buffalo. This shop carries bikes and equipment for all ages and it's located in one of the cutest waterfront towns around, filled with art galleries, restaurants, boutiques and more.
Hours: April 1-September 30: Monday-Thursday & Sunday 9 am-8 pm, Friday & Saturday 9 am-9 pm; October 1-March 31: Monday, Tuesday and Thursday 11 am-6 pm, Friday 11 am-8 pm, Saturday 9 am-8 pm, Sunday 9 am-6 pm

Party Animals

Sensational Birthday Celebrations
Party Necessities

When we were writing this book we had not planned on including this section. However, one thing became clear from all the moms we spoke with—everyone wanted ideas, tips and information for their child's next birthday party. Since both Sam and Simon were relatively young, neither of us had much experience when it came to this subject, but we approached the research enthusiastically, figuring it would benefit us as much as we hope it does you.

First of all, we should mention that practically any place that has classes *(gym, dance, music)* or specialized activities *(arts & crafts, sports)* also has some sort of birthday party package. So, if your child absolutely adores a particular class, you may want to have her birthday there.

After a while though, you may feel like every weekend is spent sitting in the same primary-color painted room, singing the same songs, doing the same activities, and eating the same pizza and birthday cake. The good news is that, if you're looking to do something a little more original for your child's birthday, you are limited only by your imagination.

For some young ones, a birthday is treated as an epic celebration that can literally become a three-ring circus. *(Seriously, you can arrange for live animals to come to your house for pony rides and petting zoos.)* On a slightly smaller scale, you can arrange to have in-home entertainment, ranging from clowns or magicians to singers or scientists. You can even get Elmo or the Powerpuff Girls to show up, if you and your child are so inclined.

Sam, being a summer baby, has had backyard barbecue parties that both kids and adults enjoy. The mess was kept outside, there was ample room for the kids to run around, and Laura just kept her fingers crossed that it wouldn't rain. It is a good idea to have some sort of centralized activity so that the children are occupied. At Sam's second birthday a singer *(whose services were won at a silent auction)* delighted the kids with music, interactive songs and small instruments for them to play. When Laura had asked the songstress to play for an hour, she just laughed. She knew that even the best performer can only captivate a very young crowd for about half an hour. Don't plan on a one-hour mini-concert, only to be disappointed that most children have abandoned the singer for something they deem more interesting, like stepping on ant hills.

Simon is a winter baby whose first big celebration *(his bris)* was disrupted by a monumental blizzard. Well, you can't control the weather, but for all you "control freaks" out there here's a story you'll enjoy. For Simon's second birthday Betsy *(a self-proclaimed "Type A" personality)* had ordered all the supplies several months ahead of time, addressed envelopes every time she got a free minute and filled out the invitations so they could be mailed at least a month in advance. As she chatted on the phone, she stuffed all the invites into their envelopes and stamped them. Several days after she mailed them, a stream of confused phone calls started to trickle in. It turns out that half the invitations she had mailed out were blank. Thank goodness for return addresses!

It's odd, when you consider the millions of details we all juggle on a daily basis, that throwing a simple birthday party for a preschooler can totally stress us out. That's why we asked a bunch of local moms about their favorite party spots, entertainers and activities and have listed some of the most popular

Savvy Suggestion

Never get caught scrambling for a gift again. Buy multiples of children's gifts when you find them on sale and stash them in a closet for future birthday parties.

recommendations. The one thing we've definitely discovered is that there is absolutely no correlation between how much money you spend and how much fun the kids have at the party. The other thing we've learned is that cake and pizza equals fun; if they served it at the doctor's office your kids would probably even enjoy going there.

Sensational Birthday Celebrations

ANIMALS
Stew Leonard's
1 Stew Leonard's Dr., Yonkers (914) 375-4700
www.stewleonards.com

It's two hours of non-stop action. From face painting upon arrival to visiting with the farm animals at the small zoo, the kids are kept entertained. Several of Stew's assistants help kids do an arts & crafts project, make their own sundaes, have pizza and cake, sing songs and do dances. Weather permitting, the party can be held on the outside deck by the zoo. In the colder months, there is a private indoor party room. "Wow the Cow" will also make a special appearance, but don't worry: they won't be offended if your child prefers to take a pass on their mooing mascot.
Ages: 3–8
Cost: $189.95 for 10 children *($12.95 for each additional child)*

The Nature of Things
(914) 276-3454
www.thenatureofthings.com

Your child can choose from over 160 animals for this one-hour educational, yet highly entertaining, activity. They will bring in ten to twelve animals ranging from amphibians and reptiles to insects, mammals and birds for a hands-on visit either in the comfort of your own home or at a rented facility. Parties can include songs and games, and the birthday child gets a free nature book.
Ages: 3 and up
Cost: $220–$360, depending on the number of children

ARTS & CRAFTS
Sandy Deck's Parties
300 Phillips Park Road, Mamaroneck (914) 722-4800
126 Garth Rd., Scarsdale (914) 722-4800
44 Triangle Center, Yorktown Heights (914) 962-7988
77 High Ridge Rd., Stamford, CT (203) 965-8381
www.sandydeckparties.com

They offer a large variety of party options, including: carnival, plastercraft, karaoke, sand art, jewelry and beading, tea parties, stuff-a-pet, cheerleading, games and more. They take care of everything, down to the goody bag. They also can arrange to do in-home parties.
Ages: 2–12
Cost: $300+ for 1½ hours. The price varies depending on the type of party you select.

Fun Craft
590 Central Park Ave., Scarsdale (914) 472-1748

You can choose from a wide variety of age-appropriate activities, including "create a mat" *(great for the young ones),* sand art, puppet making, plastercraft, soap making, and more. Basic parties include a deejay, cupcakes, soda, paper goods, balloons, invitations and thank-you cards, as well as goody bags. For a few dollars more you can get video games and karaoke, too. They will also arrange for food to be brought in if you'd like. There is an eight-child minimum during the week and a twelve-child minimum on the weekends.
Ages: 3–14
Cost: The basic package starts at $5.99 per child, plus the cost of the project. Most projects are $7.99–10.99 per child.

CHARACTERS
Marcia the Musical Moose
(212) 567-0682
www.marciathemusicalmoose.com

Marcia charms youngsters with guitar music, magic and puppets. The show is forty-five minutes for children ages three and under, and sixty minutes for children ages four and up.

Ages: 1–7, but best for the younger ones
Cost: $220-$250

Dave's Cast of Characters
(914) 235-7100
www.davescast.com

It seems like there is nothing Dave and his "cast" can't do.
From costumed characters to clowns to carnival games—
they do it all. Want a ball pit? An inflatable bouncy castle?
Laser tag, pony rides or pop diva look-a-likes? No problem.
Dave's staff will customize any party to meet your needs
and your guest list.
Ages: 1 and up
Cost: $295+ for 1 hour

Pinkie the Clown
(718) 822-7462 or (800) 246-PINK
www.pinkietheclown.com

The antidote for those of us with "clown issues" Pinkie is
sweet and upbeat without being the slightest bit scary. She
wears minimal face make-up and performs magic tricks,
tells age-appropriate jokes and makes balloon hats for all
the kids.
Ages: 3–8
Cost: $300 for 1 hour

COOKING
Little Cooks
(888) 695-COOK/(201) 493-9412
www.littlecooks.com

This is a party idea that really cooks! A "chef" will come to
your house and help kids whip up a main course and a
dessert. Perennial favorites include "tic-tac-toe" pizza and
cookie lollipops.
Ages: 4–14
Cost: $240 for 10 children (*$22 for each additional child*);
Includes chef's hats, aprons and ingredients.

GYMNASTICS
The Little Gym
777 White Plains Rd., Scarsdale (914) 722-0072
www.thelittlegym.com

Children can literally bounce off the walls at this gym facility. There are trampolines, swings, mats and a trained gym staff to help kids safely enjoy all the fun equipment. This may be a good option if you have a wide age-range of kids to invite. Older ones can enjoy the more advanced options while babies can roll around on the cushiony floor mats (*rest assured it's clean—no shoes or socks are allowed in the gym!*). The party package includes invitations, paper goods, pizza and cake, but you can bring in your own food as well.
Ages: 1 and up
Cost: $350 for up to 12 children (*$12 for each additional child*).

MAGICIANS
Magically Yours
(516) 677-0883
www.magic-al.com

"Magic Al" *(along with his bird, "Poopsie")* performs eye-popping illusions and sidesplitting comedy for kids of all ages. A veteran entertainer, he's a popular choice among many local celebrities and will certainly make your child feel like a star.
Ages: 3 and up
Cost: $550 for 1 hour

MOVIE THEATERS
For the slightly older set, this is a great party option. Each child gets popcorn, a drink and a chance to see a first-run movie on the big screen.

Clearview Cinemas
1 (877) KID-FUN6
www.clearviewcinemas.com

This package includes a private screening, popcorn, soda, cake, your child's name on the marquis, all necessary paper goods, and staff to help. If there is not an appropriate movie playing at the time of your child's birthday you can bring in a VHS tape of his favorite film to be viewed on "the big screen." You can also bring in your own pizza or cake. Clearview has locations in Bedford, Bronxville, Larchmont, Mamaroneck, Mount Kisco, Rye, White Plains and Yonkers.

Hours Available: Monday–Thursday 4-6 pm, Friday 3:30-5:30 pm, Saturday and Sunday 10 am–12 pm
Ages: 6 and up
Cost: Monday–Thursday, $395 for 25 kids; Friday–Sunday, $495 for 25 kids

MUSICAL ENTERTAINERS
A Joyful Noise
(914) 576-3854

Saragail Benjamin is a trained teacher and composer who will engage your children with a highly participatory performance that includes original songs, puppets, magic, dancing and more.
Ages: 1–7
Cost: $225 for 45 minutes

Sing Me a Story
(212) 501-4636
www.susanmirwis.com

Susan Mirwis is a singer and actress who will delight your child with musical storytelling, creative movement and instruments to play along.
Ages: 3–8
Cost: $200 for 45 minutes

Graham Clarke
(914) 669-5843
graham@grahamclarke.com

Silly, zany and all the rage, Graham is beloved by the preschool set. He sings songs that have kids rolling in the aisles

and works the crowd into a frenzy. He's recorded several of his own CDs, which can be given away as party favors.
Ages: 3–7
Cost: $300 for 30 minutes, $350 for 45 minutes, $400 for 1 hour

PUPPETS
Rick Stevens
(845) 691-3702
A primo puppeteer. Rick sets up a mini-theater in your home or party space and delights kids with his famous Sesame Street send-up, including a certain lovable, furry, red monster.
Ages: 2–6
Cost: $200 for 35 minutes

SCIENCE PARTY
Mad Science
(914) 948-8319
www.madscience.org

Kids take part in hands-on experiments like making tornado tubes or unlocking the mysteries of electricity, air pressure and chemical reactions. All parties end with children making their own silly putty or slime. For an additional charge, parties can include a rocket launch or a dry ice option. Plus, they prepare goody bags for you.
Ages: 5–12
Cost: $250+ for 1 hour

187

STORYTELLERS
Storytime Stage
(914) 478-4854

Erin Kelly and Nora Maher bring to life classic tales and original stories using song, movement, live guitar and lots of audience imagination and participation. They finish off their parties by making balloons sculptures for all the kids.
Ages: 2–6
Cost: $230 for 45 minutes

TEA PARTY
Sugar & Spice
(914) 788-7199

How about a spot of tea *(or pink lemonade if you'd prefer)* complete with kid-friendly finger sandwiches, real linen and china? Every party features a specific theme and party package to suit your child's interests, dress up, and a crafts project. Parties are held at your home or another location of your choice. Fran, the owner, is happy to accommodate any special requests—she once made sugar-free treats for a birthday girl who had diabetes.
Ages: 4–10
Cost: Packages start at $249 for 10 kids *($15 for each additional child)*

Savvy Superlatives

Our favorite party favors
* Have the kids decorate simple wooden frames *(from a crafts shop)* with paint pens, glitter glue, stickers and pom poms. Take Polaroid or digital photos of the kids at the party and send them home with a personalized keepsake.
* Buy plastic, kid-sized chairs and use a permanent marker to personalize them for each guest.
* Give each guest a mini-photo album. Send one or two photos of the party in the thank-you notes.
* Instead of gifts, try a book exchange. Every kid brings a wrapped book, and then every kid takes a wrapped book home.
* Burn a compilation CD of your child's favorite tunes or your party theme and give it out at the end of the party.

Party Necessities

SUPPLIES
In addition to the many independent party supply stores in the county, there are two major chains in Westchester that stock lots of goodies: **Party City**, with five locations *(Mount Kisco, Port Chester, Yonkers, Yorktown Heights and Stamford, CT)* and **Rojay** *(Mount Vernon and White Plains)*. Or, check out the following locations for your party needs.

Strauss Warehouse Outlet
140 Horton Ave., Port Chester (914) 939-3544

This discount mega-store carries everything you could need for a birthday party, and at cheaper prices than you'll find anywhere else. It's also THE place for all your Halloween needs.

Alperson Party Rentals
107 Fairview Park Dr., Elmsford (914) 592-8300
www.alpersonpartyrentals.com

If you don't happen to have seating for forty, if you're look-ing for an industrial-size coffee maker, or if you want those cute little party tables and chairs for kids, you may want to try a party rental place. Alperson will deliver and pick up items with a minimum order of $75 *(it may be more, depending on where you live)*. Otherwise, you can load up the back of your SUV with anything and everything you need to complete the perfect party.

Savvy Suggestion

For party favors, check out the personalized gifts places in Chapter 11—some of the less expensive gifts make great party favors!

WEBSITES

Going online is one of the easiest and most convenient ways of taking care of all your party needs, and you can do it from the comfort of your home. These sites let you search by theme, age, favorite characters and more. Plus, you can get everything from invitations to the goodies in your goody bag shipped directly to your front door. Now that's a reason to celebrate!

Here are a few of our favorites:

www.iparty.com

www.birthdayexpress.com

www.birthdayinabox.com

www.piñatas.com
More piñatas than you can shake a stick at! Also, for those of you who believe blindfolds and bats don't mix, they sell a pull-string conversion kit.

www.oriental.com
Wondering where to find a six-foot inflatable palm tree or pick up a dozen candy necklaces? If you've ever seen the Oriental Trading Company's catalog, you know that this is the ultimate resource for fun things that won't cost a fortune. They also have a fabulous selection of stuff for goody bags and party favors. You can also call them at (800) 875-8480.

CAKES

If you're feeling particularly ambitious, take a whirl at making your own cake. Many of the party stores listed above have fun cake molds and toppings. If you'd prefer to go the store-bought route you'll be able to get a perfectly delicious cake at your local bakery or supermarket. However, if you're looking for something just a little bit more special *(the icing on the cake, so to speak)* check out these two places.

Lexington Square Cafe
510 Lexington Ave., Mt. Kisco (914) 244-3663
www.lexingtonsquarecafe.com

This restaurant is known for more than its food. They have an eye-popping array of original creations to fit any theme and every budget. A week's notice for cakes is recommended—if you check out the cakes on their website you'll know why.

Riviera Pastry Shop
660 Saw Mill River Rd., Ardsley (914) 693-9758
www.rivierabakehouse.com

Widely regarded as the most amazing bakery in Southern Westchester, their selection of whimsical creations is staggering. For specialty cakes you must order at least a week in advance. They can get pricey, but if you want to make your child's special day a little bit more so, these incredible cakes are sure to do just that.

Stew Leonard's
1 Stew Leonard's Dr., Yonkers (914) 375-4700
www.stewleonards.com

A slightly less expensive option that doesn't skimp on the splendor. They offer a wide variety of popular character, theme and even photo cakes.

Savvy Suggestion

Brilliant Birthday Bashes *(That Won't Break the Bank)*

* Fill a piñata with pre-wrapped and labeled gifts so every guest gets the perfect prize *(an especially good idea if your guests vary widely in age)*.
* Spread "bubble wrap" on the floor. Play music and have the kids dance and stomp the bubbles.
* Have children decorate ceramic flower pots and plant a flower to take home.
* For a first birthday, ask everyone to bring something for a time capsule that the child will open on his or her 21st birthday.
* Pre-bake sugar cookies using fun cookie cutters for children to decorate with colored frosting, mini-M&Ms, sprinkles and other fun toppings *(For older kids making the cookies can be part of the festivities.)*
* Hire some neighborhood teens to help out at your party.

www.thisissohelpful.com

Local Websites
National Child-Related Websites
Local Publications
Local & National Hotlines

What did we do before the Internet? There is a ton of information to be found there—maybe too much—that can answer any question you may have. Although we've just scratched the surface, below are some of our favorite local and national websites to start you on your way. These sites will help you plan a daytrip, stay up-to-date on the County government, obtain child-related developmental and medical information, and more. We've also listed local publications and where to find them. Finally, we've listed some telephone hotlines in case you want to speak to a real, live person; these organizations will provide information and help on a variety of topics.

193

Local Websites

* www.americantowns.com—Information and events in Westchester, listed by town
* www.daytrips.org—Hudson Valley daytrips
* www.gocitykids.com/?area197—A site and newsletter with kid-friendly events and family resources in N.Y.C.
* www.hudsonriver.com—Historic River Towns of Westchester website; lists attractions and historical sites
* www.hudsonvalley.org—Historic Hudson Valley website; information on mansions, parks, etc.
* www.kidsevents.com—Online source of kids events and some class information for Connecticut and parts of NY
* www.newyork.urbanbaby.com—New York City resources and information for new parents

* www.nyc.babyzone.com—New York City information, plus articles and resources for pregnancy through parenthood
* www.parenthood.com—A national website with local listings
* www.parentsknow.com—Articles, resources and local calendar information
* www.scarsdaletoday.com—News and events in the Scarsdale area
* www.townlink.com/community_web/—Community pages, Westchester and New York State links
* www.westchestergov.com—Westchester County government website; lists news, information and events
* www.westchesterny.com—Westchester County Office of Tourism; provides listings and local events
* www.westchester1.com—Directories and listings

National Child-Related Websites

There are lots of pregnancy-, baby- and child-related websites to choose from. They offer articles, advice, information, resources, online communities and shopping. Some of the most popular and comprehensive websites of this type are:

* www.babycenter.com
* www.busyparentsonline.com
* www.iparenting.com
* www.parentcenter.com
* www.parentsoup.com
* www.thebabycorner.com

And this one deserves special mention:
www.fathersworld.com is chock-full of information, resources, support and education for fathers and their families.

And, if you're looking for health-related advice, try these sites:

* www.aap.org—American Academy of Pediatrics website
* www.kidsgrowth.com—Website developed by pediatricians, with advice and articles by topic

* **www.kidshealth.org**—Medical information geared toward children
* **www.postpartumny.org**—Postpartum Resource Center of New York website, with healthcare referrals, educational materials and support
* **www.womenshealthnetwork.org**—National Women's Health Network website, with information, articles and resources by topic
* **www.zerotothree.org**—Website focused on the development of infants and toddlers, with content provided by doctors and childcare experts

Local Publications

There are several local publications that will provide you with articles about Westchester, as well as schedules of upcoming events. Some are geared towards children and families, and some towards adults.

* **Westchester County Times**—Free, found in newspaper dispensers around the county
* **Westchester Family Magazine**—Free, found in supermarkets, schools, libraries and some kids' stores
* **Westchester Parent Magazine**—Free, found in supermarkets, schools, libraries and some kids' stores
* **Westchester Magazine**—found in some area stores, or by subscription *(for information, call (800) 254-2213 or visit www.westchestermagazine.com)*
* **Westchester Wag**—free, found in area stores

Local & National Hotlines

Hopefully you'll never need these, but you should have them at the ready just in case.

* **Domestic Violence Hotline:** (800) 942-6906
* **National Child Abuse Hotline:** (800) 422-4453
* **Poison Control Center:** (800) 336-6997
* **Public Health Hotline/Westchester County Dept. of Health:** (914) 813-5000
* **Toy Safety Hotline:** (800) 851-9955

195

Special Stuff for Special Needs

An Introduction to Early Intervention

When Betsy's son was five months old and involved in his first playgroup, she noticed that he seemed slightly delayed compared to the other kids. C'mon, say it with us: "Don't compare your child to other children. All children mature at their own rates." Okay, that's true. But in Simon's case, as the months went on, she continued to note that her son appeared to be developing a couple of months behind the other children: sitting up at nine months, crawling at twelve months, and not walking until nearly seventeen months. While none of these delays are so off the charts as to cause complete panic, Betsy consulted her pediatrician and they agreed to have Simon evaluated by a physical therapist through the New York State Early Intervention Program.

Early Intervention, or "E.I.", as it's often called, is a program offered through the New York State Department of Health that is designed to assist children ages 0–3 years with developmental delays. The services are free (*New York State attempts to get some compensation from your health insurance provider, but that's not your headache*).

If you're concerned about your child, first consult with your pediatrician. Then call the Westchester County Early Intervention Program at (914) 813-5094. No one wants to overreact, but if you are worried, don't procrastinate. The earlier you start your child in the program, the faster the problems may be resolved.

You will be assigned an E.I.O. (*an Early Intervention Official*) who will get the process rolling and set up the necessary evaluations. Once your child is evaluated, one of two things will happen: either the therapist will reassure you that your child is within the normal range of development and you have nothing to worry about, or she will pick up on some issue that, in many cases, can be successfully resolved with a little extra help from an appropriate therapist. If your child qualifies for services, therapies can take place in the home, at a daycare facility, in a classroom or at a center designed especially for developmental therapies.

Neither of us are doctors or child development specialists, but having gone through E.I., Betsy has become well versed in the basics of the program. Here are descriptions of some of the many professionals and services that Early Intervention can provide:

Family Trainer: Provides parental support and often acts as a therapist for the parents, since they may have difficulty at times dealing with their child or with their child's special needs. The trainer meets alone with the parent, rather than with the child.

Feeding Specialist: Often a speech therapist or nutritionist with a specialty in this area. Feeding therapy may be needed if your infant is having difficulty or discomfort feeding (either by breast or bottle), or if your child is having problems chewing and/or swallowing or is perhaps not eating at all.

197

Occupational Therapist (O.T.): Often the "catchall" therapy, An O.T. is used particularly to improve "fine motor skills" (the ability to use hands for manipulation, coordination and smaller, more refined tasks). Also widely used in treating Sensory Integration Dysfunction (S.I.D.).

Physical Therapist (P.T.): This type of therapist usually addresses issues of "gross motor skills" (that is, large muscle functions like crawling, standing, walking, balance and over-all coordination).

Special Educator or Special Instructor: Has a background in Special Education and/or Social Work. Through the use of play therapy, they work with your child on cognitive skills and on social and emotional development. Their goal is to help the child reach her full potential in the areas of learning and interacting with the environment.

Speech Therapist: Can be used to treat speech delays and oral motor issues *(such as excessive drooling)*, and to improve articulation and interpersonal language skills.

When your child reaches the age of three he is eligible to transition to a different program, called Preschool Special Education Services *(C.P.S.E.)* This program assists children ages 3–5 within the school environment. Its services are offered by the New York State Education Department through your local school district.

For more information about the Early Intervention Program or to receive a copy of the Early Intervention Family Resource Directory, contact:

Early Intervention Program
Bureau of Child and Adolescent Health
New York State Dept. of Health
Corning Tower, Rm. 208
Albany, NY 12237-0618
(518) 473-7016
www.health.state.ny.us

Other resources that may be helpful are:

"Growing up Healthy" 24-Hour Hotline
(800) 522-5006

New York Parent's Connection
(800) 345-KIDS

Early Intervention is an incredible program. The best advice we can give you is this: if you have even the slightest concern regarding your child's development, you should talk to your pediatrician about getting in touch with the Program to set up an evaluation.

Simon is an E.I. success story. He began at thirteen months and will be finished with most of the therapies this summer, when he is three-and-a-half years old. His progress has been remarkable, and he has formed close bonds with all of his therapists. By getting the extra support he needed early on, he may not have to struggle further down the road and, as any mother knows, that's the greatest thing of all.

To Your Health

Hospital Directory

The last time most of us were in the hospital we left with a little bundle of joy. And many of us picked the hospital by default— it was where our obstetrician worked. However, there may be times in the future when a trip to the emergency room is required. You should make it a point to know where the closest hospital to you is and the quickest way to get there. We listed all the area hospitals below to help you.

Savvy Suggestion

If your trip to the emergency room is not for a life-or-death situation, consider going to a smaller hospital that might be just a bit further away. The emergency wards tend to be less busy, so you may not need to wait for hours, as you might during peak hours in a larger facility.

BRONXVILLE
Lawrence Hospital
55 Palmer Ave. (914) 787-1000
www.lawrencehealth.org

CORTLANDT MANOR
Hudson Valley Hospital
1980 Crompond Rd. (914) 737-9000
www.hvhc.org

DOBBS FERRY
Community Hospital at
Dobbs Ferry
128 Ashford Ave.
(914) 693-0700

HARRISON
St. Vincent's Hospital
Westchester
275 North St.
(914) 967-6500
www.svcmc.org/westchester

KATONAH
Four Winds Hospital
800 Cross River Rd. (914) 763-8151
www.fourwindshospital.com

MOUNT KISCO
Northern Westchester Hospital Center
400 E. Main St. (914) 666-1200
www.nwhc.net

MOUNT VERNON
Mount Vernon Hospital
12 N. Seventh Ave. (914) 664-8000

NEW ROCHELLE
Sound Shore Medical Center of Westchester
16 Guion Pl. (914) 632-5000
www.ssmc.org

OSSINING
Stony Lodge Hospital
40 Croton Dam Rd. (914) 941-7400
www.stonylodgehospital.com

PORT CHESTER
New York United Hospital Medical Center
406 Boston Post Rd. (914) 934-3000
www.uhmc.com

Savvy Suggestion

If more than a couple stitches are needed, do not be shy about requesting a plastic surgeon to do the honors—they're usually able to minimize scarring.

RYE
Rye Hospital Center
754 Boston Post Rd. (914) 967-4567
www.ryehospitalcenter.org

SLEEPY HOLLOW
Phelps Memorial Hospital Center
701 N. Broadway (914) 366-3000
www.phelpshospital.org

VALHALLA
Blythedale Children's Hospital
Bradhurst Ave. (914) 592-7555
www.blythedale.org

Westchester Medical Center
95 Grasslands Rd. (*Valhalla Campus*) (914) 493-7000
www.wcmc.com

WHITE PLAINS
St. Agnes Hospital
305 North St. (914) 681-4500
www.stagneshospital.org

White Plains Hospital Center
41 E. Post Rd. (914) 681-0600
www.wphospital.org

YONKERS
St. John's Riverside Hospital
967 N. Broadway (914) 964-4444
www.riversidehealth.org

St. Joseph's Medical Center
127 S. Broadway (914) 378-7000
www.saintjosephs.org

Yonkers General Hospital
2 Park Ave. (914) 964-7300

CONNECTICUT
Danbury Hospital
24 Hospital Ave., Danbury (203) 797-7000
www.danburyhospital.org

Greenwich Hospital
5 Perryridge Rd., Greenwich (203) 863-3000
www.greenhosp.org

Norwalk Hospital
Maple St., Norwalk (203) 852-2000
www.norwalkhosp.org

ROCKLAND COUNTY
Nyack Hospital
160 N Midland Ave., Nyack (845) 348-2000
www.nyackhospital.org

Savvy Suggestion

If you and your spouse are traveling out of town you might consider signing over temporary power of attorney to whoever is caring for your child. Should consent for a medical procedure be necessary, this will speed up the process.

For a quick and inexpensive way to get this and other legal documents in order, go to:

We The People
148 Mamaroneck Ave. White Plains (914) 683-5105
www.wethepeopleusa.com.

There are over eighty document preparation services that customers can choose from, including wills and trusts, incorporations, bankruptcies and power of attorney.

Westchester Suburbs Simplified

Cities, Towns, Villages & Hamlets

Westchester is a confusing puzzle of cities, towns, villages and hamlets, many of which overlap in one way or another. The real estate listings are full of riddles like homes with a Yonkers address but a Bronxville P.O. Depending on where you live, these strange arrangements can have an impact on which schools your children attend, who provides your municipal services *(garbage collection, etc.)*, how high your taxes are and which swimming pool you're allowed to use. While writing this book, Betsy and Laura, for example, lived less than a half a mile apart in Hartsdale, which is governed by the Town of Greenburgh—but Betsy's school district was Edgemont *(ranked #1 in the county)*, while Laura's was Greenburgh *(significantly lower in the rankings)*. For your information, we've provided the following list of Westchester's cities, towns *(with their hamlets)* and villages, as well as contact phone numbers and websites, where available.

Cities

MOUNT VERNON
(914) 665-2300
www.cmvny.com

NEW ROCHELLE
(914) 654-2000
www.newrochelleny.com

PEEKSKILL
(914) 737-3400
www.peekskill.americantowns.com

RYE
(914) 967-9371
www.ryeny.gov

WHITE PLAINS
(914) 422-1200
www.cityofwhiteplains.com

YONKERS
(914) 377-6000
www.cityofyonkers.com

Towns

BEDFORD
(includes the hamlets Bedford Hills and Katonah)
(914) 666-6530
www.bedfordny.info

CORTLANDT
(includes the hamlets Crugers, Montrose and Verplanck)
(914) 734-1000
www.townofcortlandt.com

EASTCHESTER
(914) 777-3300
www.eastchester.org

GREENBURGH
(includes the hamlets Fairview, Glenville, Greenville and Hartsdale)
(914) 993-1540
www.greenburghny.com

HARRISON
(includes Purchase and West Harrison)
(914) 835-2000
www.town.harrison.ny.us

LEWISBORO
(includes the hamlets Cross River, Golden's Bridge, Lewisboro, South Salem, Vista and Waccabuc)
(914) 763-3511
www.lewisborogov.com

MAMARONECK
(914) 381-7805
www.townofmamaroneck.org

MOUNT KISCO
(914) 241-0500
www.mountkisco.org

MOUNT PLEASANT
*(includes the hamlets Hawthorne, Pocantico Hills,
Thornwood and Valhalla)*
(914) 742-2300
www.mtpleasantny.com

NEW CASTLE
(includes the hamlets Chappaqua and Millwood)
(914) 238-4771
www.town.new-castle.ny.us

NORTH CASTLE
(includes the hamlet Armonk)
(914) 273-3321
www.northcastleny.com

205

NORTH SALEM
*(includes the hamlets Croton Falls, Peach Lake, Purdys and
Salem Center)*
(914) 669-5110
www.northsalemny.org

OSSINING
(914) 762-6000
www.townofossining.com

PELHAM
(914) 738-1021
www.townofpelham.com

POUND RIDGE
(includes the hamlet Scotts Corners)
(914) 764-5511
www.townofpoundridge.com

RYE
(914) 939-3553
www.townofryeny.com

SCARSDALE
(914) 722-1100
www.scarsdale.com

SOMERS
(includes the hamlets Amawalk, Croton Falls, Golden's Bridge, Granite Springs, Lincolndale, Purdys, Shenorock and Somers)
(914) 277-3323
www.somersny.com

YORKTOWN
(includes the hamlets Crompond, Croton Heights, Huntersville, Jefferson Valley, Kitchawan, Mohegan Lake, Shrub Oak, Sparkle Lake, Teatown, Yorktown and Yorktown Heights)
(914) 962-5722
www.yorktownny.org

Villages

ARDSLEY
(in Greenburgh)
(914) 693-1550
www.ardsleyvillage.com

BRIARCLIFF MANOR
(in Ossining and Mount Pleasant)
(914) 941-4800
www.briarcliffmanor.org

BRONXVILLE
(in Eastchester)
(914) 337-6500
www.villageofbronxville.com

BUCHANAN
(in Cortlandt)
(914) 737-1033

CROTON-ON-HUDSON
(in Cortlandt)
(914) 271-4781
www.village.croton-on-hudson.ny.us

DOBBS FERRY
(in Greenburgh)
(914) 693-2203
www.dobbsferry.com

ELMSFORD
(in Greenburgh)
(914) 592-6555
www.elmsfordny.org

HASTINGS-ON-HUDSON
(in Greenburgh)
(914) 478-3400
www.hastingsgov.org

IRVINGTON
(in Greenburgh)
(914) 591-7070
www.village.irvington.ny.us

207

LARCHMONT
(in Mamaroneck)
(914) 834-6230
www.ci.larchmont.ny.us

MAMARONECK
(in Mamaroneck and Rye)
(914) 777-7700
www.village.mamaroneck.ny.us

MOUNT KISCO
(in Mount Kisco)
(914) 241-0500
www.mountkisco.org

OSSINING
(in Ossining)
(914) 762-8428
www.village.ossining.ny.us

PELHAM
(in Pelham)
(914) 738-2015
www.villageofpelham.com

PELHAM MANOR
(in Pelham)
(914) 738-8820
www.pelhammanor.org

PLEASANTVILLE
(in Mount Pleasant)
(914) 769-1900
www.pleasantville.americantowns.com

PORT CHESTER
(in Rye)
(914) 939-5202
www.portchesterny.com

RYE BROOK
(in Rye)
(914) 939-1121
www.ryebrook.org

SCARSDALE
(in Scarsdale)
(914) 722-1100
www.scarsdale.com

SLEEPY HOLLOW
(in Mount Pleasant)
(914) 366-5100
www.sleepyhollowny.org

TARRYTOWN
(in Greenburgh)
(914) 631-7873
www.tarrytown.americantowns.com

TUCKAHOE
(in Eastchester)
(914) 961-3100
www.tuckahoe.com

quick guide

Select Listings By Location

219

WEBSITES

notes

notes

notes

notes